The Battle of Bussaco

WELLINGTON AT BUSSACO

The Battle of Bussaco

27th September, 1810, Between
Wellington's Anglo-Portuguese Army and the
French Army Under Masséna

ILLUSTRATED

G. L. Chambers

LEONAUR

The Battle of Bussaco
27th September, 1810, Between Wellington's Anglo-Portuguese Army and the French
Army Under Masséna
by G. L. Chambers

ILLUSTRATED

Leonaur is an imprint of Oakpast Ltd

Copyright in this form © 2019 Oakpast Ltd

ISBN: 978-1-78282-882-2 (hardcover)
ISBN: 978-1-78282-883-9 (softcover)

http://www.leonaur.com

Contents

DEDICATED TO

THE RIGHT HONOURABLE EARL ROBERTS

P.C., K.P., G.C.B., G.C.S.I., G.C.I.E.,V.C., K.G., D.C.L., LL.D. ETC.

WHO WAS GOOD ENOUGH TO CONVEY HIS KIND PERMISSION IN THE
FOLLOWING TERMS:

It is most interesting, and a very valuable account of the Battle of Busaco. I shall be very pleased to have such a book dedicated to me. The illustrations and photographs lend a special value to the work.

Bussaco.

'Twas here, e'en here, brave Lusitania
Her path to glory found once more,
'Twas here the tyrant's eagle cowering wept
In dust her mighty arm before.

Hear'st thou the cry of vanquish'd men, the din
Of battle, and deep-mouth'd cannons' bray?
Hear'st how the clarion's far re-echoed note,
Lost in the distance, dies away?

Then hail! majestic shades of those who fell
For Portugal! Upon mine ear
It is your triumph-song the forest sings,
Your elegy methinks I hear.

Nay, sleep on now, ye gallant hearts, sleep on
In valour's vast and restful room:
To this old land the morn of Liberty
And Life, beams brightly from your tomb.

Translated from Luiz Carlos, by the Rev. R. H. Chambers, M.A., Christ' College, Brecon.

Preface

There are many people living who remember the time when everybody knew all about the Duke of Wellington and the Peninsular War, but a generation is now springing up, or rather has sprung up, of which the majority knows little and cares less about the Great Duke and his campaigns.

On the other hand, I find a great number of people on both sides of the Atlantic who are so much interested therein as to read every available book on the subject.

Amongst these are, of course, to be found large numbers of soldiers—for the Peninsular Wars were wars in which strategy had an all-important part—while the display of tactics was of no mean order.

I do not propose to put before the reader my views on strategy in these campaigns, and only occasionally do I intend to allude to tactics. My object is to make available good plans of the battles accompanied by views illustrative of the important points. Some histories give the plans more or less correctly, and others give views, but what is wanted nowadays is a judicious mixture of both plans and views.

Some will, perhaps, think this an easy matter. I can assure them it is not so, as witness the failures made by those who do not take the trouble to master the subject of any particular battle before beginning their photographs. I have before me as I write, several photos of an important battlefield, taken by a gallant colonel, and published in the history of one of the regiments highly distinguished in the action.

I have no hesitation in stating that most of them do not represent the true locality of the event described.

Each battlefield requires careful study of the actual events which took place, of the plans available, and of the ground itself. It is also necessary to make enquiries regarding any changes that have been made, since the battle, in the roads, and to compare the old maps with modern maps, if available.

The hasty historian, the ordinary tourist, and the professional photographer, do not do these things.

Some knowledge of the languages of the countries visited is also necessary, but, above all, some sort of military training is essential. In this latter respect I can only claim long service in the volunteers in England and in India, which I have supplemented by continuous study on the spot, of the battlefields of India, Belgium, the Crimea, and the Peninsula.

I regret that I never until lately thought of using a camera in my visits to the above scenes, but I do not now neglect this important aid, and I humbly place before the reader some of the results of recent work in Portugal.

Some of my military friends who have kindly examined my photographs assure me that from them they have derived quite new ideas of the battles in question, owing to their being able to see what the ground was really like.

As regards the narrative accompanying the pictures, I have generally followed Napier and others, where I have found them practically correct, as at Roliça and Vimiero: but in the case of Bussaco, I had to write the whole account over again, in the light of special information, and of diaries and biographies published during the last sixty or seventy years.

A recent writer on the Peninsular War has done a good deal in this respect, and has succeeded in making a most readable history, though, in my humble opinion, one not free from error when describing actual battles and battlefields. He has, however, brought to light a mass of valuable information for which military and political students should be, and no doubt are, thankful, and which the general reader will find most interesting.

Note.—Prof. Oman's work is here alluded to, of which, up to now, three volumes have been published.

Laithfield, Welwyn,
September, 1910.

CHAPTER 1

The Period Preceding the Battle

The Battle of Bussaco was fought on the 27th September, 1810, between the British-Portuguese Army, under the command of Lord Wellington, and the French "Army of Portugal," under Masséna (Prince d'Essling).

Napoleon had ordered Masséna to enter Portugal and "drive the English leopard into the sea." Before the advance Marshal Ney was, however, to secure the line of communications by reducing the fortresses of Ciudad Rodrigo on the Spanish, and Almeida on the Portuguese side, of the frontier. Ney was jealous of Masséna, and was very leisurely over this, and the time he wasted had a very ill effect on the subsequent operations.

On the 1st June, 1810, however, he descended from the hills with 50,000 men, and threw his bridges over the Agueda, and on the 25th the French batteries opened their attack on Ciudad Rodrigo. The defence by the Governor, General Herrasti, a Spanish officer of advanced age, was highly creditable, and further delayed the French invasion of Portugal.

Wellington watched for a favourable opportunity of relieving the town, but none occurred. He dared not take any great risk of a reverse, as such would almost certainly have led to the withdrawal of the British Army from Portugal by the Home Government.

Ciudad Rodrigo held out until the 11th July, 1810. On the 24th, General Craufurd, commanding the British outposts on the Coa River, hardily remained too long on the French side of the Coa, and narrowly escaped defeat, all quite contrary to Wellington's orders. The latter, however, supported him, on the ground that he had acted to the best of his judgment, and said very little about the matter. The French, moreover, got rather the worst of the affair in the end, through trying

11

THE CONVENT AND HOTEL AT BUSSACO.

Little can be seen in this picture of the Convent, which is on the left front. The Grand Hotel overshadows it. The battlefield is some distance to the front of the picture.

to do too much.

Ney's corps and the Reserve cavalry remained in positions round Almeida, but the place was not yet practically invested, as Masséna was waiting for Mortier's co-operation. The latter entered Zafra near the end of July, and the 6th Corps then formally invested Almeida.

Wellington immediately brought up the Portuguese Army to Celorico, Goves, Melho, and Trancoso, while the British troops occupied Pinhel, Freixadas, and Guarda.

In these positions, expecting a vigorous defence of Almeida, he hoped to delay the enemy two months, when the near approach of the rainy season would give him further advantages in the defence of the country.

In the middle of August Ney broke ground in front of Almeida, having received the siege-train, and on the 26th the batteries were completed, and opened fire, but without serious effect. At 7 p.m. a dreadful disaster occurred. While powder was being taken out of the magazine, a French shell fell near the door, and ignited a train of powder left by a leaky barrel, causing the magazine to explode. A large part of the town defences was destroyed, and numerous gunners killed, resulting in the capitulation of the place, prematurely, on the 27th August.

In consequence, Wellington began to withdraw his army, leisurely, further into Portugal. He was not pressed by Masséna, who was short of transport and food for his troops—and did not advance until the 15th September.

On the 21st September the main body of the French entered Viseu, and found a deserted town, and on this date the whole of Wellington's army was brought into touch by the arrival of General Hill from the Castello Branco side, where he had been confronting Reynier, until the latter marched to join Masséna.

As it was most probable Masséna would advance on Coimbra by the Chamusca-Ponte Murcella road, Wellington had prepared a defensive position on the Alva, but, probably because Masséna knew this, he marched by the Viseu-Mortagoa route. As soon as he was committed to this road, Wellington made his arrangements to block his advance at the Bussaco ridge, but kept a wary watch on the movements of the enemy.

It was a nice operation, because Masséna might have changed his route at the last moment. Wellington was, however, kept well informed by his British scouting officers, and detained Hill on the south of the

GENERAL ROWLAND HILL

Mondego until it was absolutely necessary to call him in. Even on the 23rd September Wellington thought a French force might be sent across above Ponte de Murcella.

On the 24th September there was a small skirmish in front of Mortagoa, and on the 25th the Light Division was compelled to retire, *via* Moira, to the Bussaco ridge, this retirement being personally directed by Wellington.

Hill crossed the Mondego and arrived on the ridge on the morning of the 26th, and the concentration was complete.

(*General Rowland Hill* by Edwin Sidney & Alexander Innes Shand is also published by Leonaur.)

CHAPTER 2

On the Objects of the Two Commanders

Wellington's immediate plan was to delay Masséna's march on Lisbon, and to induce Masséna to attack him in some strong position, in order that the Allied Army might gain a victory with the least possible loss to themselves. He had prepared one such position on the River Alva, of which Masséna knew, and therefore avoided. Masséna's maps, and his Portuguese adherents, deceived him as to Bussaco, and Wellington's stand there took him by surprise. Masséna expected no battle north of Coimbra, because he thought Hill could not join Wellington in time. Wellington, however, thought Masséna would attack at Bussaco, and said that such an attack would be repulsed. He knew his position could be turned by the Karramulla defile, and had arranged for Colonel Trant to block it with the Portuguese Militia; but Trant's superior Portuguese officer (Baccellar) had given subsequent conflicting orders, and only a small force was available for this purpose.

The possible discovery by Masséna of this passage through the Karramulla, or Boilva Pass, was the only weak point in Wellington's defence. He has left on record a letter, (4th October, 1810, to Rt. Hon. W. W. Pole), in which he complains of his orders not being carried out (*vide* Appendix).

Trant did his best, and managed to interview Wellington, at Bussaco, on the 28th September, but it was quite impossible for him, with his weak and inefficient militia, to delay such an army as Masséna's for more than a few hours at the most, and it is difficult to see how Wellington could have expected him to do so, at such short notice. It might have been different if he could have had plenty of time to destroy the bridges and break up the roads in the Pass.

ARTHUR WELLESLEY, 1ST DUKE OF WELLINGTON

It is evident that Wellington thought it inadvisable to detach any part of his own army to the western end of the Pass, being already weaker than his adversary. Lord Burghersh, *Early Campaigns in Portugal and Spain*, says:

> Wellington had been extremely anxious for the arrival of Trant. This road by Sardao was the only Pass by which the position of Bussaco could be turned, and there were parts of it so extremely difficult that if this corps of militia had had the necessary time to destroy the bridges, and to avail itself of the positions afforded by the ravines, which intersect the road, it might have opposed a most decisive resistance to the advance of the enemy.

Judging, however, from the conduct of Trant's force, I do not believe Masséna would have been delayed long by it, and certainly would not have been forced to turn back and fight Wellington again at Bussaco. Wellington, however, thought he would either be obliged to do so, or return to Spain (*vide* his letter to the Earl of Liverpool dated 3rd November, 1810, and his letter of the 4th October, 1810, to the Right Hon. W. W. Pole, both of which will be found in the Appendix).

No doubt Wellington was right in his opinion as to what Masséna *ought* to have done, but, as he shows in the above letter of the 3rd November, 1810, Masséna was *not* guided by correct military principles in persisting in his advance beyond the Mondego after his reverse at Bussaco; and it appears to me, therefore, that the same obstinacy, which impelled him to disregard these true principles, would have induced him to force his way through the Karramulla defile, even if Trant had succeeded in destroying the bridges, and had attempted any defence of the defile with such wretched troops as he commanded at that time.

It was not any great advantage, from a strategical point of view, to repulse Masséna, unless it should lead him to retire from Portugal; Wellington has said that he expected Masséna to retreat after the defeat, and he showed anger when the French columns were seen making for the defile on their right rear.

But even if Masséna did not retreat, the advantage of a victory over him was immense, for political reasons. It would not only affect the Portuguese, Spanish and British Governments, but would be felt all over the Continent, amongst the wavering nations.

Wellington was not only weakly supported by the British authorities, but was at variance with the Peninsular Governments. The former were actually expecting him shortly to embark for England with the British Army.

If, then, Masséna could not be so severely beaten as to make him withdraw from Portugal, there is little doubt that from the strategical standpoint, a leisurely retirement to the lines of Torres Vedras, leaving a devastated country to the French, would be equally effective, without a battle. The actual advantages of victory would be only political, and we may say tactical, for, if the Portuguese fought well, they would gain confidence in themselves, and secure the respect of their allies, which would be practical advantages in future operations.

As a matter of fact, the concentration of Masséna's army for battle at the commencement of Wellington's retreat on Torres Vedras had disadvantages for the Allies which were not properly availed of by the French, and Masséna's neglect, especially in not making a rapid advance, *via* Tentugal, enabled them to make a comparatively secure retreat. One of the objects which, it is said, Wellington had in view in making a stand at Bussaco, was to gain time to destroy his magazines at and near Coimbra, which he could not remove. He did not succeed altogether in doing this, but the French got little advantage, as the soldiers wasted most of what was left.

Masséna's object was simple. His orders were to drive the British Army into the sea, and recapture Lisbon. The plan of campaign had been sketched out by Napoleon. Masséna was to capture the frontier fortresses, so as to secure his base, and attack the British wherever they were, and force them to embark. Both Napoleon and Masséna fully expected that this would be easily accomplished. They knew Wellington's British Army was outnumbered by three to one, and the value of the Portuguese troops they regarded as "nil." Even after Bussaco, the French were not undeceived in this respect, for we find Junot gravely stating that Wellington had dressed up British soldiers in Portuguese uniforms to deceive the French, which matter is referred to hereafter.

Napoleon knew nothing of the existence of Wellington's fortified lines of Torres Vedras, nor of his arrangements for the devastation of the country and removal of the inhabitants to Lisbon.

Masséna only learnt of the lines after his army left Coimbra, and did not realise their importance until he actually saw them.

CHAPTER 3

Composition of the Two Armies

The Anglo–Portuguese Army, concentrated at Bussaco to resist the further advance on Lisbon, *via* Coimbra, consisted of 52,272 men, while that of the French was 62,462 strong.

Prof. Oman, in his *History of the Peninsular War,* gives the details as follows:—

ALLIES.

	British.	Portuguese.	Total.
Infantry	24,777	24,549	49,326
Cavalry (somewhat understated)	210	—	210
Artillery	1,350	880	2,230
Engineers	43	—	43
Waggon train	422	—	422
Staff corps	41	—	41
Present	26,843	25,429	52,272
Not present, but within 20 miles	2,919	1,450	4,369
	29,762	26,879	56,641

FRENCH.

Infantry	49,986	Total French	
Cavalry	8,119	Army	65,974
Artillery, Train, Engineers	6,656	Not present	3,512
Marines	924	Present	62,462
État-Major	289		
	65,974		

20

Masséna was, therefore, superior in numbers to the extent of 10,190 men, and his troops were all as of one nation, accustomed to act together, and mostly veterans.

The Portuguese troops were not at that time well trained, and had seen practically no service, besides being half starved by their Government.

The 8,000 French cavalry were only used as a reserve, but would have been useful if the Allies had left their stronghold. The English troopers (4th Heavy Dragoons), 210 in number, were posted in the centre, near the highest point of the ridge, and another detachment of the 16th Light Dragoons was behind Craufurd.

The French Artillery was sparingly used—Masséna, or his generals, overrated the difficulties of the ground, which they had only cursorily examined.

Reynier's attack would have been more dangerous if he had risked bringing up a strong force of guns—but the carriages had been very hardly used by the roads of Portugal, and were in bad order—and the English engineers had broken up the roads, so that they would have had to advance the guns over ground strewed with rocks. In attacking, Masséna relied on his superiority in infantry, but the extraordinary strength of the position, and the judicious mixture of the Portuguese with British troops by Wellington, combined to render an attack exceedingly hazardous.

CHAPTER 4

Position of the Anglo-Lusitanian Army

The Allied troops were posted on the 27th September, at the moment of attack, as follows:—

On the extreme right of the ridge—

The 2nd Division—Gen. Hill (not engaged).

Brigade A. Col. Duckworth (acting).

			Officers.	Men
3rd foot	1st Batt.	..	32	826
31st ,,	2nd ,,	..	27	384
48th ,,	2nd ,,	..	27	454
66th ,,	2nd ,,	..	30	433
60th Rifles 1 Co. 5th Batt.			1	33
			117	2130 = 2247

Brigade B. Col. Inglis.

			Officers.	Men.
29th Foot ..	..	..	31	430
48th ,,	1st Batt.	..	32	519
57th ,,	1st ,,	..	28	727
60th Rifles 1 Co. 5th Batt.			1	50
			92	1,726=1,818

Brigade C. Col. Wilson.

			Officers.	Men.
28th Foot 2nd Batt.		..	32	522
34th ,,	2nd ,,	..	36	617
39th ,,	2nd ,,	..	27	394

60th Rifles 1 Co. 5th Batt.   2   42

                        97   1,575 = 1,672

                                5,737

Note.—The above brigading is taken from an article by C. F. Atkinson in *English Historical Magazine*, Vol. XVII, p. 124.

HAMILTON'S PORTUGUESE DIVISION.

(Attached to 2nd Division under Gen. Hill.)

Lt.-Col. Arch. Campbell's Brigade.

				Officers and Men.	
4th Line	2 Batts.	..		1,164	
10th ,,	2 ,,	..		1,086	
					2,250

Brig.-Gen. Fonseca's Brigade.

2nd Line	2 Batts.	..		1,317	
14th ,,	2 ,,	..		1,373	
					2,690
		Total		10,677	

General Hill's Division was not engaged with the enemy in the battle, but Lieut. Fox, of the 2nd Battalion, 66th Regiment, was killed. On the morning of the 27th they were under arms two hours before daybreak, and were disposed on the ridge, with their extreme right, consisting of A. Campbell's Portuguese Brigade, on the slope overlooking Penacova. The left of A. Campbell's Brigade was on the Coimbra route Carvalbal-Caval.

Next on the left of this road, which can still be traced, came Fonseca's Brigade. Further to the left on higher ground were the British brigades of Duckworth, Inglis, and Wilson.

Wellington had given orders that if Leith and Hill were not attacked, or threatened, by the enemy in their front, they should move to their left. When, therefore, Leith moved to succour Picton's Division, Hill followed and took up a position to the right of the S. Antonio Pass.

The 5th Division (Maj.-Gen. Leith) consisted of—

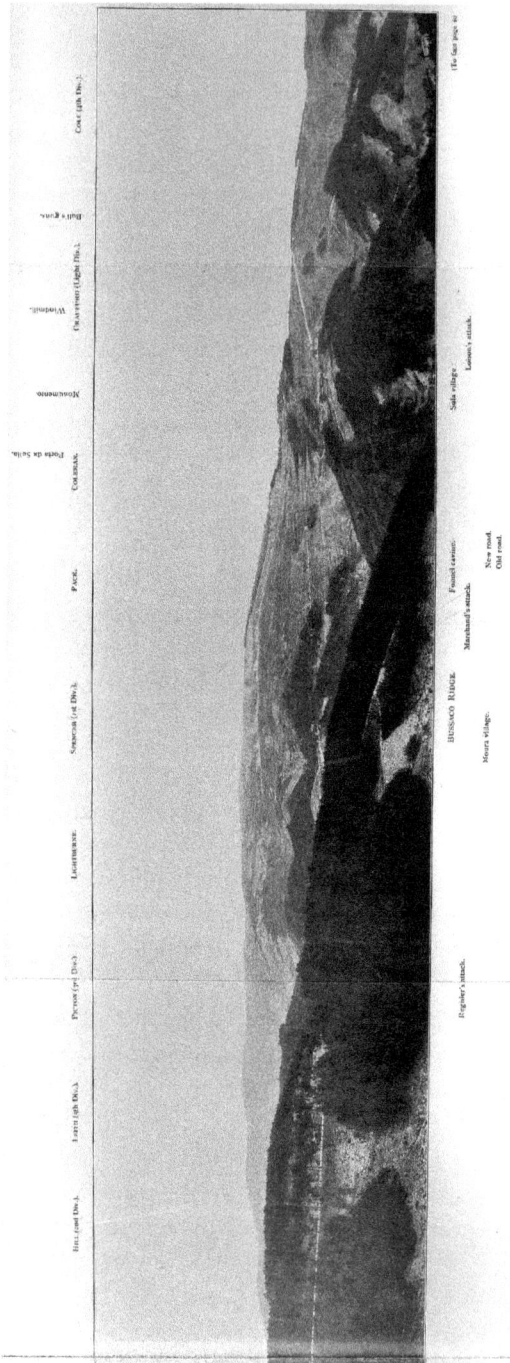

BESSACO RIDGE.

Lt.-Col. Barnes' Brigade.

	Officers.	Men.
Maj. Gordon, 1st Foot (Royals), 3rd Batt.	35	733
Lt.-Col. Cameron, 9th Foot, 1st Batt.	30	585
Lt.-Col. Nugent, 38th Foot, 2nd Batt.	29	467
	94	1,785 = 1,879

Brig.-Gen. Spry's Portuguese Brigade.

	Officers and Men.	
3rd Line, 2 Batts.	1,134	
15th ,, 2 ,,	905	
		2,039
The Thomar Militia (attached) Col. Baron Eben.	580	
Lusitanian Legion, 3 Batts. Col. Douglas.	1,646	
8th Line 2 Batts.	1,161	
		3,387
Total	7,305	

At the commencement of the action the British troops belonging to Gen. Leith's Division were next in position to Gen. Hill's Division, and were astride the S. Paulo-Palmazeo road. On their left, nearly a mile away, the Lusitanian Legion was placed on a hill opposite Carvalhos. Nearly another mile to the left was Spry's Portuguese Brigade, while the 8th Portuguese were behind the hill commanding the S. Antonio do Cantaro Pass.

Of Gen. Leith's troops, the 9th and 38th Foot and the 8th Portuguese were engaged with the enemy, and did good service, and the 1st Royals were exposed to fire.

A defect of the above arrangement was that the 8th Portuguese (2 battalions) were completely separated from Gen. Leith. They were under the command of Col. Douglas, and Major Birmingham commanded one of the battalions. As these troops were helping to defend the S. Antonio Pass, which was entrusted to General Picton, it would seem that they came altogether under his orders, and he sent part of them away to the left of the Pass when necessity arose.

On the left of Gen. Leith's troops, the next in order consisted of—
The 3rd Division (the Fighting Division), Maj.-Gen. Picton.

Lieutenant-General, Sir Thomas Picton

Col. Mackinnon's Brigade.

	Officers.	Men.
Lt.-Col. Meade, 45th Foot, 1st Batt.	35	560
Lt.-Col. Trench, 74th Foot, 1st Batt.	38	456
Lt.-Col. Wallace, 88th Foot, 1st Batt.	40	679
	113	1,695 = 1,808

Lightburne's Brigade.

5th Foot	2nd Batt.	..	..	31	464
83rd ,,	2nd ,, ..	..	..	43	461
3 Cos. 5th/90th Foot		..	..	16	145
				90	1,070 = 1,160

Col. de Champalimaud (Harvey), Portuguese Brigade.

	Officers and Men.
Lt.-Col. Sutton, 9th Line, 2 Batts. ..	1,234
Lt.-Col. Baccellar, 21st Line, 1 Batt. ..	541
	1,775
Total	4,743

Of the above, the 45th, 74th, and 88th Foot, and the 9th and 21st Portuguese, were actively engaged with the enemy. The 60th Foot (Rifles) belonging to this division were broken up, and the companies attached to other divisions, where they were actively engaged. The three companies of the 90th Foot do not appear to have been engaged, as they had no losses.

The light companies of the 5th and 83rd Foot were thrown out as skirmishers down the slope, in front of Lightburne, and lost a few men in Merle's attack. Lightburne's Brigade had been taken away from Picton, who was ordered to detach it to the high ridge, where it was posted at the side nearest to Picton—below where the new carriage road from the Porta da Sulla makes its return bend to the reverse side of the ridge, on its way to the Porta da Cruz Alto. It was above the spot to which Wellington opportunely brought the two guns of Thompson's which aided in the defence against Merle's attack.

Captain Thompson's brigade of six guns was broken up—four guns remained in the plateau to the left, near Lightburne.

The 1st Division—Lt.-Gen. Sir B. Spencer—was on Lightburne's left.

Major Sturgeon says the order was—

on (left)		(right)
Pakenham	Cameron	Stopford

Pakenham's Brigade.

			Officers.	Men.
7th Foot	1st Batt.	..	26	843
79th ,,	1st ,,	..	38	885
			64	1,728 = 1,792

Cameron's Brigade.

			Officers.	Men.
24th Foot	2nd Batt.	..	30	338
42nd ,,	2nd ,,	..	23	391
61st ,,	1st ,,	..	36	648
1 Co. 5th/60th Rifles		..	3	47
			92	1,424 = 1,516

Stopford's Brigade.

		Officers.	Men.
1st Coldstream Guards	..	24	790
1st Scots Fusilier Guards	..	26	791
1 Co. 5th/60th Rifles	..	2	51
		52	1,632 = 1,684

Total	4,992

Spencer's Division held the highest part of the ridge, Cameron in centre, Pakenham on the left, and the Guards on the right. Their front was well protected by a steep slope covered with boulders and stones, and their left rested on the convent wall. Their skirmishers were thrown out to their front, and had numerous vantage points amongst the rocks and broken ground. They were engaged for a long time with the Voltigeurs, and lost a good many men.

On the right rear of the Guards were two squadrons of the 4th Dragoons, 210 in all.

The northern wall of the convent enclosure was an important part of Wellington's scheme of defence, although actually not made use of. An opening appears to have been made at the corner near Pakenham's Brigade—where the wall touched its highest point—but no record seems to have been made anywhere as to how it was fortified. At the Porta da Sulla, lower down, the entrance was covered by an abattis, staging was erected inside the enclosure, on both sides of the gate, for infantry to fire from over the wall, whilst the wall itself was lowered considerably, and loopholed there and elsewhere. Many of these holes remain unclosed to this day.

On the left front of Spencer's left brigade, on a lower slope, above the right part of the "funnel ravine" was posted—

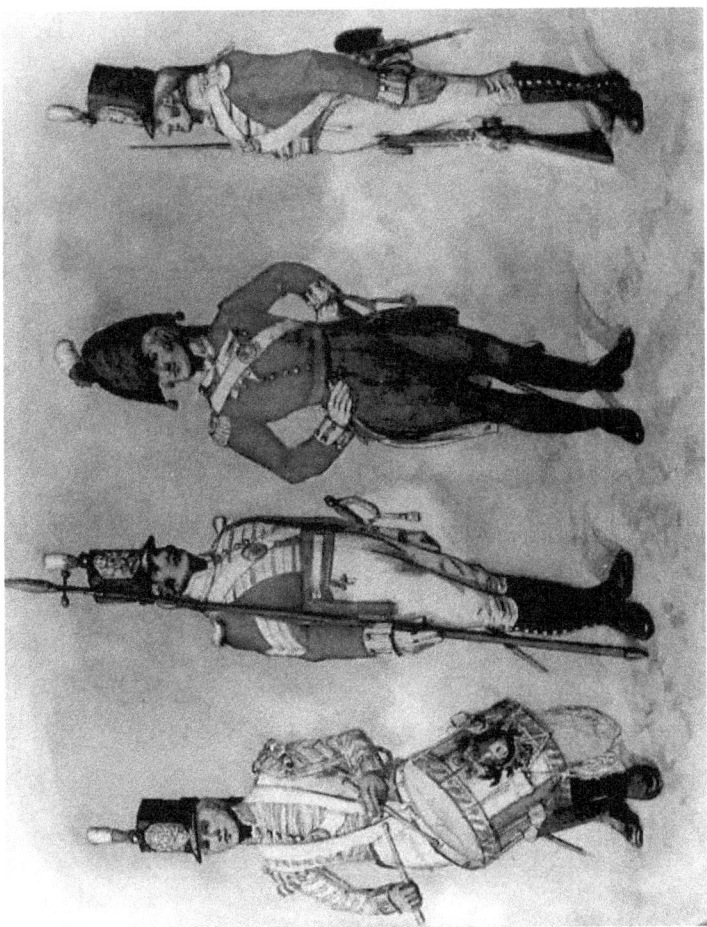

BRITISH INFANTRY

Brig.-Gen. Pack's Independent Brigade of
Portuguese.

	Officers and Men.
Lt.-Col. Hill, 1st Line, 2 Batts. ..	1,089
Major Armstrong, 16th Line, 2 Batts.	1,130
Col. Don L. de Pegoa, 4th Caça-	
dores, 1 Batt.	550
	2,769

This brigade, by its fire, aided by the artillery, repulsed Marchand's Brigade, all the regiments being
engaged.

Next was the LIGHT DIVISION—Gen. Craufurd.

Lt.-Col. Beckwith's 1st Brigade.

	Officers.	Men.	
Lt.-Col. Macleod, 43rd Foot,			
1st Batt.	40	804	
Major Gilmour, 95th Rifles,			
4 Cos.	12	384	
Lt.-Col. Elder, 3rd Caçadores		656	
	52	1,844	= 1,896

*Lt.-Col. Barclay's * Brigade.*

	Officers.	Men.	
Hon. Major Arbuthnott, 52nd			
Foot, 1st Batt.	29	946	
Major Stewart, 95th Rifles, 4 Cos.	12	358	
Lt.-Col. Davelais, 1st Caçadores		546	
	41	1,850	= 1,891
			3,787

* He was severely wounded, and died in May, 1811.

The Light Division occupied a ridge which formed a sort of natural fort, having on its right rear a small plain with a gentle slope, and in
its front a steep descent, difficult to mount except by the road, owing
to its being covered with irregular blocks of stone, covered partly with
low scrub, but nowhere giving any cover. The left part of it was nearly
impassable at one steep, rocky place. The ridge was of such a shape
that troops on the reverse side, yet near the crest, could be completely
hidden from the view of an enemy approaching from Sula, or any part
of the front.

The ridge faced the French, except that it took a bend round to
the right, where it overlooked the "funnel ravine." This will be seen

Major-General Craufurd

from the photographs.

All Craufurd's troops were actively engaged.

Behind Craufurd, to his right rear, near the convent wall, was—

The 6th Independent Portuguese Brigade, under
Brig.-Gen. Coleman.

	Officers and Men.
7th Line, 2 Batts.	815
Lt.-Col. McBean, 19th Line, 2 Batts.	1,124
2nd Batt. Caçadores	406
	2,345

The 19th Regiment (one battalion) successfully charged a stray battalion, belonging probably to Ferey; and the *caçadores* must have been engaged, as they lost 43 men killed, wounded, and missing, or about 11 *per cent* of their number.

The King's German Legion was posted, according to Napier, a quarter of a mile behind the Light Division, on the high ground near the convent wall, but Prof. Oman places them, in his plan of the battle, about 1,000 metres to the left rear of Craufurd, on the opposite side of Monte Novo.

I have been unable to discover any authority for this, and I follow, therefore, Napier and the maps published after the battle. It seems more than doubtful, moreover, whether Prof. Oman gives the correct position of the Light Division. I should place Craufurd further to the left, and the Legion further to the right, than the Professor does, which would agree with Napier's History better, and with other authorities.

Lowe's Brigade.

	Officers.	Men.
1st Line Batt. K.G.L. ..	28	510
2nd ,, ,, ,, ..	31	453
5th ,, ,, ,, ..	30	460
7th ,, ,, ,, ..	24	429
Detachment Light Batts. K.G.L.	6	90
	119	1,942 = 2,061

The King's German Legion relieved the Light Division after Loison's attack, and in skirmishing about Sula lost a number of men belonging to their light companies; which were engaged on both the 26th and 27th September. In the early morning of the 27th a detach-

32

THIS SHOWS THE REVERSE SIDE OF THE WINDMILL HILL, WHICH THE
LIGHT DIVISION OCCUPIED. THE KING'S GERMAN LEGION WAS POSTED
ON THE SLOPE TO THE LADY'S LEFT.

ment of these riflemen was nearly cut off by the advancing French columns.

On the continuation of Craufurd's ridge, to his left, was posted—

The 5th Independent Brigade of Portuguese,
under Brig.-Gen. A. Campbell.

				Officers and Men.
6th Line	2 Batts.	..	..	1,317
18th ,,	,,	..	..	1,386
6th Batt. Caçadores		..	..	546
				3,249

When the Light Division moved forward against Loison's Division, A. Campbell's Brigade took ground to their right. The 6th and 18th Line were not actively engaged, but the 6th Caçadores had 23 casualties when skirmishing.

Still further to the left was placed the 4th Division, under General Cole.

Alex. Campbell's Brigade.

			Officers.	Men.	
7th Foot	2nd Batt.	..	29	585	
11th ,,	1st ,,	..	42	920	
53rd ,,	2nd ,,	..	25	448	
5th/60th Rifles, 1 Co.		..	2	58	
			98	2,011 =	2,109

Kemmis' Brigade.

27th Foot	3rd Batt.	..	34	785	
40th ,,	1st ,,	..	48	1,007	
97th ,,	..	..	27	493	
5th/60th Rifles, 1 Co.		..	4	50	
			113	2,335 =	2,448

Collins' Portuguese Brigade.

11th Line	2 Batts.	..	..	1,438	
23rd ,,	,,	..	..	1,405	
					2,843
	Strength of 4th Division		..		7,400

(The above numbers of officers and men are all taken from Prof. Oman's work.)

Kemmis's and Alex. Campbell's British Brigades came next in order to A. Campbell's Portuguese, and were on a continuation of Craufurd's ridge—while Collins' Portuguese Brigade was on the extreme

Cole.

Craufurd..................

The Reverse side of Cole's and Craufurd's Positions.

†††
Bull.

†††
Ross.

43rd and 52nd Regiments this side of the crest.

left, somewhat more advanced.

Four (so-called) roads led over or past the Ridge of Bussaco.

(1) On the right of the Allied position was the junction of the high roads from Gondolem and Carvalhos, which cross the Serra do Bussaco as one.

(2) The S. Antonio do Cantaro Pass road.

(3) The Moura-Sulla road past the convent wall.

(4) On the extreme left of the position there was a practicable track, partly covered by Gen. Cole's Division, running parallel with the convent road, to the low country, via Villa Nova (*vide* Appendix).

There was also a road by which the position could be turned via Mortagoa and Boialva, which was discovered by Masséna after the battle.

The nature of the position selected by Wellington will best be understood by an examination of the photographs accompanying this work. The whole position was eleven miles long. The ridge is highest in the centre, which of itself is a very strong position. The constant references in books on the Peninsular War to crags and precipices are not reliable; these are not to be found on any large scale.

The advantage of the position lay in its top being *alternately* narrow and fairly broad, with a steep slope on the French side nearly everywhere, and in the fact that all the movements of the French were discernible, while the bulk of the Allied troops could be hidden from view until wanted.

In addition to this, the French guns were at a disadvantage in having to pass over roads previously broken up by the English Engineers. Moreover, there was no good lateral road for the French guns to use, and their gun-carriages were already in very bad order.

French writers also complain that their guns had to fire upward at concealed enemies, while the Allied guns had not these disadvantages.

The whole of the ridge and its sides are strewn with both large and small boulders and outcropping rocks, while dwarf brushwood and heather made marching difficult and tiring to the French troops.

Wellington had taken the precaution of making a good lateral road along the ridge before the battle. The peasants and Portuguese Caçadores were employed on this under the direction of the English Engineers.

This shows the village of Moira in the background, and is taken from below the Porta da Sulla, looking down the "funnel ravine." Head-quarters of Masséna during battle.

Entrances were made in the convent wall to allow of the troops entering quickly, and for their obtaining fuel, and about half the eastern wall was thrown down from the top of it to the centre, so as to admit of the Allied troops firing over it, while a large part of it was loop-holed. At the Porta da Sulla a battery was constructed inside the entrance, to which guns could be brought if necessary, and the gate itself was defended by an oak abattis. Stages were erected there for the troops to stand on, and fire over the wall.

The Porta da Rainha on the north side was found closed with stones, and was opened. Altogether six entrances were made available for entrance into the convent enclosure.

Bussaco Serra is often referred to as the Iron Ridge. The origin of this may be due to the fact that the red stone found there is full of iron, and there are small mines all along the ridge. There is no granite there, as stated by Prof. Oman and other writers.

The red conglomerate certainly looks to an ordinary observer something like granite, and some of the other rocks found there are probably nearly of the same age as granite.

Since going to press the following further names of officers commanding regiments at Bussaco have been ascertained :—

2nd/31st Foot	. .	Lt.-Col. John William Watson.
2nd/48th ,,	. .	Major Brooke.
2nd/66th ,,	. .	Captain Kelly.
2nd/39th ,,	. .	Major Patrick Lindesay.
2nd/5th ,,	. .	Lt.-Col. The Hon. Henry King.
2nd/83rd ,,	. .	Lt.-Col. Collins.
1st/7th ,,	. .	Brevet Lt.-Col. Blakeney.
2nd/7th ,,	. .	Lt.-Col. Sir William Myers.
1st/79th ,,	. .	Lt.-Col. Philips Cameron.
1st/11th ,,	. .	Major Newman.
2nd/53rd ,,	. .	Lt.-Col. Bingham.
3rd/27th ,,	. .	Lt.-Col. John Maclean.

Near the convent at Bussaco

CHAPTER 5

The Position of the French Army

It will not take long to describe the position of the French Army—
the strength of the corps is taken from returns in the Archives Nation-
aux at Paris, given in Prof. Oman's work.

Reynier's, *i.e.* the 2nd Corps, was at and about the village of S.
Antonio do Cantaro, opposite Picton's Division.

It consisted of—

MERLE'S, THE 1ST DIVISION.

Sarrut's Brigade.

			Officers and Men.	
2nd Leger	4 Batts.	..	2,358	
36th Ligne	4 ,,	..	2,076	

Graindorge's Brigade.

4th Leger	4 Batts.	..	2,155	
				6,589

HEUDELET'S, THE 2ND DIVISION.

Foy's Brigade.

17th Leger	3 Batts.	..	1,398	
70th Ligne	4 ,,	..	2,458	

Arnaud's Brigade.

31st Leger	4 Batts.	..	1,768	
47th Ligne	4 ,,	..	2,463	
				8,087

The Cavalry Brigade of P. Soult.

(In rear of the above Infantry.)

		Officers and Men.
1st Hussars		
22nd Chasseurs ..		
8th Dragoons		1,397
Hanoverian Chasseurs		
Artillery, Train, and Engineers		1,579

40

État-Major   66

2nd Corps—Total   17,718

THE 6TH CORPS, commanded by Marshal Ney, was stationed round Moira. It consisted of the following troops :—

1ST DIVISION. Gen. Marchand.

Maucune's Brigade.

6th Leger	2 Batts.	..	1,478
69th Ligne	3 ,,	..	1,717

Marcognet's Brigade.

39th Ligne	3 Batts.	..	1,686
76th ,,	3 ,,	..	1,790

6,671

2ND DIVISION. Gen. Mermet.

Bardet's Brigade.

25th Leger	2 Batts.	..	1,715
27th Ligne	3 ,,	..	1,886

Labasses' Brigade.

50th Ligne	3 Batts.	..	2,121
59th ,,	3 ,,	..	1,894

7,616

3RD DIVISION. General Loison.

Simon's Brigade.

26th Ligne	3 Batts.	..	1,625
Legion du midi	..	..	564
Legion Hanoverienne, 2 Batts.			1,158

Ferey's Brigade.

			Officers and Men.
32nd Leger	1 Batt.	..	413
66th Ligne	3 Batts.	..	1,830
82nd ,,	2 ,,	..	1,236

6,826

Cavalry Brigade. General Lamotte.

3rd Hussars	..	}	1,680
15th Chasseurs	..	}	
Artillery, Train, Engineers	..		1,431
État-Major	..	..	82

6th Corps—Total   24,306

THE 8TH CORPS, commanded by Gen. Junot, was stationed in reserve behind Moira. It took no part in the battle.

1ST DIVISION. Gen. Clausel.

Brigade Menard—19th, 25th, 28th, |
            and 34th Ligne |

,,   Taupin—15th Leger, 46th ⎞   6,794
            and 75th Ligne   ⎟
,,   Godard—22nd Ligne ..   ⎠

2ND DIVISION. Gen. Solignac.

Brigade Gratien—15th & 86th Ligne ⎞
,,   Thomières—65th Ligne   ⎟
Regiment Irlandais   ..   .. ⎬   7,226
,,   de Prusse   ..   ..   ⎠
CAVALRY DIVISION. Gen. St. Croix.

1st, 2nd, 4th, 9th, 14th, 26th Dragoons
(two squadrons of each)   1,863
Artillery, Train, and Engineers   ..   981
État-Major   75

            8th Corps—Total   16,939

The *Reserve of Cavalry*, under General Montbrun were placed about a mile to the left rear of Moira. They consisted of the—

                                     Officers and Men.
Brigade Lorcet—3rd, 6th Dragoons   ⎞
,,   Cavrois—11th Dragoons   ⎬   3,179
,,   Ornano—15th,25th Dragoons   ⎠
Horse Artillery   300

                                        3,479

Not attached to any Corps.

Artillery Reserve,Train, and Engineers 2,365
Gendarmerie   ..   ,.   ..   177
État-Major   66
44th Equipage de Marine   ..   924

                                    3,532

The Total Army would then add up as follows :—

2nd Corps   17,718
6th Corps   24,306
8th Corps   16,939
Reserve of Cavalry   3,479
Sundries   3,532

        Masséna's Army   65,974
Less Sick, Stragglers, etc.   ..   3,512

        Actually present   62,462

Against Wellington's Army of 52,272

42

Chapter 6

Battle Tactics

Before entering upon a description of the actual attacks made by the French, we will refer to the battle tactics on which each side at this period relied for success.

The French attack on a position was usually made by compact columns, which were intended by their formidable aspect to impress their adversaries, and by their weight to break through the defence, their advance being covered by clouds of skirmishers. Wellington knew this would be the method adopted if he was attacked.

It was a matter about which he had made up his mind long ago. It is recorded somewhere that before leaving India he had said that as British troops only could fight successfully in line of two deep, he hoped in Europe, if he was placed in high command, to gain victories by the use of "line "formations, as opposed to those of "columns."

The divisional generals made the actual dispositions for meeting the French attacks, but the battle tactics employed were the result of long and careful consideration by Wellington.

Attacks in column being then looked for, the tactics on the side of the Allies consisted in endeavouring to repulse them:

(1) By the free use of skirmishers, sufficiently strong in numbers to deal effectually with those of the enemy.

(2) By artillery fire from guns trained on vital points at known ranges, firing round shot or shrapnel, or both, as considered best, and placed where possible in flanking positions.

(3) By the concealment of reserves, and consequent surprise.

(4) By frontal and flank fire, in the later stages of the attack, of troops in line formation.

(5) By a bayonet charge against the columns when rendered helpless by the disorder caused by the foregoing means.

In all cases of attack in column, the question is whether the column can retain its order, under such harassing conditions as the above, long enough for it to close with the line formation. If it can do this, there is little doubt that it can pierce the line. The French had been usually successful in closing with the troops of other nations, but only the British soldiers had at this time the hardihood to withstand column attacks when in line of two deep, partly from their natural disposition, and partly from their superior skill in the use of their weapons.

Over and over again in the Peninsular War, and as late as Waterloo, was this exemplified.

At Roliça and Vimiero, and at Bussaco, the Allies had a great advantage, owing to the use of Col. Shrapnel's spherical case-shot by the British Artillery against masses of the enemy.

It had a longer range than similar French missiles. In some cases, at Bussaco the English gunners loaded with both round shot and shrapnel.

As regards musketry fire, the British had a marked superiority. Up to this time they were the only troops perfectly practised in the use of small arms, their light troops were the best marksmen in Europe, and their riflemen had the best rifles.

There is a good illustration of this given in Colonel Willoughby Verner's *A British Rifleman*.

A French officer asked an Englishwoman in Lisbon to admire his beautiful company of Frenchmen, and asked her whether there were such beautiful troops in the English Army. She replied that there were, but he said he had a very poor opinion of the military value of English infantry. This officer was wounded at Vimiero, and was brought to the English lady's house. He then said:

> I met the English. Oh! that morning was one of the most happy of my life. My men, to a man, had the same feeling. I was sent out to skirmish against some of them in green, grasshoppers I call them, you call them riflemen. They were behind every bush and stone, and soon made sad havoc amongst my men, killing all the officers of my company, and wounding myself, without our being able to do them any injury. This drove me nearly to distraction.

Another matter showing different ideas of tactics was the way in

44

which Wellington and French generals respectively took up positions.

Had a French general been in possession of Bussaco he would probably have shown where all his troops were posted, presumably to encourage his own side, and to impress the enemy.

Wellington knew better—he showed his troops as little as possible. His great object was to conceal his men, especially the reserves (see Note, below).

He thus provided surprises for the enemy, and prevented them from judging correctly where his weak points were.

Masséna is reported to have expressed an opinion, after reconnoitring Wellington's position, that the Bussaco ridge was only occupied by a strong rear-guard.

Masséna was at some disadvantage in making observations, however, as he had only one eye, and was a bad rider. He was therefore dependent on the reports of others, with many of whom he was on bad terms.

He is reported to have said on the 26th September:

I cannot persuade myself that Lord Wellington will risk the loss of his reputation by giving battle; but if he does, I have him! Tomorrow we shall effect the conquest of Portugal—and in a few days I shall drown the Leopard.

★★★★★★

Note.—At Waterloo Wellington did not show his whole force, a large part being in line behind the crest of the hill. This surprised Napoleon, and on his making a remark about it to Gen. Foy, who spoke from experience, the latter is said to have answered:

"Wellington conceals his troops until they are needed, but your Majesty will see them in due time. They are the devil in close fight."

"*Allons donc*," replied the Emperor, "*nous verrons.*"

★★★★★★

45

CHAPTER 7

The Night Before the Battle

The French troops were well supplied with firewood and water, but they were very short of provisions, and were living on oranges, and maize which they found in the fields.

The English and their Allies were well supplied with food, but were not allowed to light fires, so that both sides passed a more or less uncomfortable night.

Wellington slept at the convent, in his room with two doors, for which he had stipulated, and had to take the smallest in consequence. The *Diary* of Fr. José gives some interesting particulars of the convent life at this period.

Wellington's army had no tents in the campaigns prior to that of 1813-14, and the nights at this season of the year are cold, and dews and mists prevail, but the Allies, no doubt, were too anxious about the morrow to think much of the inconveniences of their situation.

The British troops were very doubtful of the value of the Portuguese, and despite their strong position, many, even of the officers, were dubious of the result of the coming contest.

The author of *Recollections of the Peninsula* thus relates his thoughts and feelings on first seeing the French Army. He was an officer in Hill's corps:—

My regiment had no sooner piled arms than I walked to the verge of the mountain on which we lay, in the hope that I might discover something of the enemy. Little, however, was I prepared for the magnificent scene which burst on my astonished sight. Far as the eye could stretch, the glittering of steel, and clouds of dust raised by cavalry and artillery, proclaimed the march of a countless army; while immediately below me, at the feet of those precipitous heights on which I stood, their picquets were already posted: thousands of them were already halted in their bivouacs, and column too after column, arriving in quick succession, reposed upon the ground allotted to them, and swelled the black and enormous masses.

The numbers of the enemy were, at the lowest calculation, 75,000, and this host formed in three distinct and heavy columns; while to the rear of their left, at a more considerable distance, you might see a large encampment of their cavalry, and the whole country behind them seemed covered with their train, their ambulance, and their commissariat.

This, then, was the French Army: here lay before me, the men who had once, for nearly two years, kept the whole coast of England in alarm; who had conquered Italy, overrun Austria, shouted victory on the plains of Austerlitz, and humbled in one day, the pride and the martial renown of Prussia, on the field of Jena.

Tomorrow, methought, I may for the first time, hear the din of battle, behold the work of slaughter, share the honours of a hard-fought field, or be numbered with the slain. I returned slowly to the line, and after an evening passed in very interesting and animated conversation, though we had neither baggage, nor fires, we lay down, rolled in our cloaks, and with the stony surface of the mountain for our bed, and the sky for our canopy, slept or thought away the night. Two hours before break of day, the line was under arms: but the two hours glided by rapidly and silently. At last, just as the day dawned, a few distant shots were heard on our left, and were soon followed by the discharge of cannon, and the quick, heavy, and continued roll of musketry.

General Picton, with the 3rd Division, known as the "Fighting Division" afterwards, was stationed on the S. Antonio do Cantaro Pass road, where it crosses the Sierra da Bussaco range.

The following story is taken from Robinson's *Life of Picton*:

The night was cold, and the position occupied by the troops exposed them to the inclement blast which swept over the mountains: even the hardy veteran shrank within his scanty covering. The young soldiers, however, and even the young officers, endured with less patience their mountain couch. A party of these latter (to one of whom we are indebted for this anecdote) tired of the coldness of their situation, resolved to try whether the enemy were equally inactive.

Accordingly, Capt. Urquhart, with Lieuts. Tyler, Macpherson, and Ousely of the 45th, walked down the steep slope towards the advanced posts occupied by the enemy, and arrived at a spot whence the artillery had been withdrawn only a short time previously. Here they found some straw, which offered so strong a temptation to obtain a few minutes' repose that each ensconced himself beneath a heap, and prepared to enjoy his good fortune. They were soon fast asleep: even the roll of the drums was unheeded, and the first sound that broke their rest was the clash of bayonets.

This ominous sound effectually roused them, and they scampered back to their regiment with admirable expedition—a retrograde movement which was accelerated by a strong impression that they could hear the enemy coming up the hill. Upon reaching their line they found the regiment formed, and silently waiting the attack. To fall in without being observed by the Colonel (Meade) was out of the question. They had long been missed, and he had sent orderlies in all directions for them: and he now pounced upon them, as they approached, full of this encroachment upon military discipline. He loudly called to them:

'There you are! I'll report every one of you to the general: you shall all be tried for leaving your ranks while in front of the enemy!'

Observing at this moment that they were attempting to fall in and avoid further castigation, he assailed them with renewed eloquence: 'Stop, sirs, stop! Your names—for every one of you shall be punished. It's desertion.' And a great deal more he would have added, but the French were on the move, and each officer having given his name without waiting for any further observations occupied his post in the ready formed ranks, much chagrined at the unfortunate event of their expedition and its probable result.

But the fight soon began, and every other thought was absorbed in the heat of battle. After the enemy had been repulsed the firing ceased, and the Allies were falling back upon Coimbra, Colonel Meade, who was a severe disciplinarian, and possessed a most inveterately good memory, resolved to fulfil his promise, and report the offending officers to General Picton. Seeing Lieutenant Macpherson, he called to him, and in a tone of severity, said:

'Well, sir, you remember last night, I suppose?'

Macpherson bowed with no very enviable recollections.

'Ah, it's a breach of discipline not to be forgotten,' continued the colonel, with a stern and uncompromising look. 'Where is Urquhart?'

'Killed,' replied the lieutenant.

'Ah,' grunted out the disciplinarian, 'it's well for him. But where is Ousely, sir?'

'Killed, sir,' again responded Macpherson. (Ouseley was quite a boy, and in carrying out some order about the pickets accidentally got between the French and the English and was killed.)

'Bah!' exclaimed the colonel, in a still louder tone, as if actually enraged at thus being deprived of the opportunity to punish their breach of military discipline. As a last resource, however, he enquired:

'Where is Tyler?'

'Mortally wounded, sir,' was the reply. This was too much for the old colonel's patience, so, with a look of anger, he rode off, leaving his only remaining victim in a state of much uncertainty. Two days afterwards, Macpherson received a message from his friend Tyler, who, with the rest of the wounded, had been carried into Coimbra, requesting to see him; he applied to Colonel Meade for leave, stating at the same time that his object in doing so was to attend, as he thought, the dying moments of his friend.

'No, no,' said the colonel, 'you shan't go, you haven't deserved it, sir. Go to your duty.'

Macpherson shortly after this met General Picton, and to him he stated the request which his chum Tyler had made and Colonel Meade's refusal to grant him leave. Picton was indignant.

'What, not let you go?' he exclaimed, in his usual forcible and energetic manner. 'Damn me! you shall go, and tell Colonel Meade I say so, d'ye hear, sir?'

The young lieutenant both heard and obeyed. Thanking the general, he set off, first to deliver Picton's message to the infuriated colonel, who swore that 'all discipline in the army had ceased,' and then to Coimbra, where he found his friend Tyler not dead, nor dying, but wonderfully recovered from the severe wound he had received, and prepared with an excellent breakfast for Macpherson and some more of his companions, whom he had contrived to allure into a participation of the good cheer he had provided, by the invitation to attend his dying moments. ((*Picton* by H. B. Robinson and John Cole also published by Leonaur.)

With regard to the gallantry displayed by the 45th Regiment, to which Tyler and his friends belonged, it may here be mentioned that Lord Wellington pardoned four men of the regiment, under sentence of death for highway robbery, in consideration of the splendid behaviour of their comrades in the Battle of Bussaco on the 27th September.

But we must return to the night before the battle.

In the *Memoirs of Marshal Saldanha*, who was then a major in the 1st Portuguese Infantry Regiment, in Gen. Pack's Brigade, it is observed that:—

His regiment was commanded by Lt.-Col. Hill; the brigade was stationed at the foot of the hill (*i.e.* below the rocky crest of the high plateau), and on the 27th the attack of the enemy commenced before dawn in that direction.

It was on the night of the 26th that Joao Carlos and a brother officer, Capt. Macintosh, were at their posts awaiting the expected attack. Saldanha, wrapped in his cloak, laid himself on the ground, and told his orderly to call him if the enemy showed any signs of movement.

"What," said Macintosh, "will you be able to get to sleep? I don't think I can."

"I hope I shall," was the reply.

The firing had commenced when the orderly called his officer, who, on waking, called out, "Halloa, Macintosh, get up."

But poor Macintosh was a lifeless corpse, near the side of his comrade—being one of the first killed in the attack.

In the *Recollections of a Subaltern*, (republished by Leonaur as *The Subaltern* by Robert Gleig), we read:

At night we lay down to rest, each man, with his firelock in his grasp, remained at his post, awaiting the arrival of the morrow, which was destined to be the last many amongst us were to behold. We had no fires, (this must have been unpleasant in

50

more ways than one, as on the Serra were many snakes), and the deathlike stillness that reigned throughout our army was only interrupted by the occasional challenge of an advanced sentry, or a random shot fired at some imaginary foe. Some of us sat together chatting over the past, and guessing as to the future: it was impossible not to regard the scene below us with feelings of awe.

An army of 65,000 to 70,000 warriors, just returned from the conquest of Germany, covered with trophies, and commanded by officers inferior to none, lay within cannon-shot of us, their demeanour, too, argued a confidence in themselves which characterises the French soldier above any other in the world: more than a thousand fires illuminated their camp, and we could perceive them in groups, either sitting round their blaze, or performing their ordinary avocations with that *sang-froid* which alone belongs to men accustomed to danger.

BATTLE OF BUSSACO

CHAPTER 8

General Sketch of the Battle

Masséna's plan of attack on the Allied position was that Reynier should advance against what was believed to be the Allied right, at, and to the north of, the S. Antonio do Cantaro Pass. His intention was that Reynier should drive the Allies towards the convent, while Loison was to follow up by an attack on the Allied left centre, situated at and near the Moira–Luzo road, *i.e.* near the village of Sula.

The attacks by Reynier are divisible into three, *viz*.:

(1) The attack on the actual Pass by the 31st Regiment.

(2) The attack by Graindorge and Sarrut on Picton's left.

(3) The attack by Foy on Picton's centre.

The attacks by Loison are divisible into two, *viz*.:

(1) The attack by Simon and Ferey on Craufurd.

(2) The attack by Marchand on Pack.

As regards Reynier's attacks. No. 1 was kept off by the fire of the infantry at the Pass, and by that of the artillery stationed there. The French were not able to press it home, and were eventually completely driven back by an advance of the Allies. No. 2 attack was defeated by the 88th and half the 45th Regiments under Wallace and Gwynne, and the 8th Portuguese, directed by Picton. No. 3 was principally disposed of by Leith with the 9th British, aided generally by the 38th Regiment, 1st Royals, and the 74th Highlanders, and by one battalion of the 8th Portuguese, under Douglas. It is possible too that the other half of the 45th Regiment, under Meade, stationed in the rocks, gave some assistance by their fire.

As regards the attacks of Loison. No. 1 was defeated by Craufurd's skilful use of the 1st and 3rd Caçadores and the 95th Regiment as

BATTLE OF BUSSACO

skirmishers, but principally by the 43rd and 52nd Regiments concealed near the crest of the hill up which the French advanced. No. 2 was kept off by the fire of Pack's Portuguese, and of the artillery.

A minor attack between Craufurd and Pack was disposed of by the 19th Portuguese (1 battalion only), who advanced down the ravine on Craufurd's right and drove the French to the bottom of it.

Thus, the French were unsuccessful everywhere. In the principal attacks their columns were smothered by the fire of the Allied troops in line, were charged by the latter with the bayonet, and driven completely off the hillside with immense loss.

The various attacks will be dealt with in detail hereafter.

CHAPTER 9

The Attacks at and Adjacent to the S. Antonio Do Cantaro Road through the Pass

PICTON'S EXTREME LEFT.

From rocky point on 2-gun knoll looking towards High Serra, on which Spencer was posted.

ALLIED SIDE.

The easy slope in front of False Pass, which descends evenly to nearly the village of S. Antonio do Cantaro. On the right is seen the rocky point A. Merle's columns crossed this slope when turned to their left by the two guns of Lane's Division.

The first point threatened by Merle's attack—or the False Pass—
commanded by the guns on 2-gun knoll.
Below is visible the so-called village of S. Antonio do Cantaro.

FRENCH SIDE.

ALLIED SIDE.

2-gun knoll—below which Merle's columns were turned by the fire
of two guns of Thompson's Battery.

The French under Merle probably marched partly on the road shown.

The rocky point on 2-gun knoll. The probable position of Wellington and staff during part of Merle's attack.

The south slope of 2-gun knoll, showing the kind of ground the French had to advance across.

It was occupied by the 88th Regiment on the evening of the 26th September, with pickets on the French side, i.e. to right of picture.

ALLIED SIDE.

A, OR CONNAUGHT ROCKS.

The scene of the struggle between three companies of the 88th Regiment
and the French tirailleurs.

From Lightburne's position looking over 2-gun knoll; further on is the rocky ridge running to the true S. Antonio do Cantaro Pass, where there is a break. Further on in the distance are the original positions of Leith and Hill. The two guns (Captain Lane) were placed on the left of 2-gun knoll rocky point. Merle's troops gathered in the ravine below the left of the picture.

Photo taken in a mist.

FRENCH SIDE.

ALLIED REAR.

S. Antonio False Pass: taken from the road of communication on the left rear of Pass. It shows A and B rocky points. A is in centre of picture. B is on the right side.

Note.—I call this the False Pass because the local guide took me and others there when I asked for the S. Antonio do Cantaro Pass. This saved the local guide an extra walk of two miles, but caused me no end of trouble.

Taken from near village of S. Antonio do Cantaro—looking at (French) right of 2-gun knoll, which is seen at left of picture. Merle advanced at left side of this picture nearly as far as 2-gun knoll and then turned to his left. Lightburne was posted about the centre of this picture, on the top.

High Serra.

White ra-
vine in
which
Merle
assembled
his troops.

Light-
burne's
Br gade.

2-gun
knoll.

26th Sept, 33th Regt.

A.

Sarrut's Defeat.

B.

Grain-
dorge s
Defeat.

C.

Foy's
Defeat.

Merle's Division.	Heudelet's Division.

4 Regts. 36th Line } Sarrut.
4 Regts. 2nd Leger }
3 Regts. 4th Leger Graindorge
(killed)
	Foy's Brigade Arnaud's Brigade.
	                                 REGTS.
	                 47th Line 3
	3 Regts. 4 Regts. 31st Leger 4
	17th Leger, 70th Line.

Merle's Division.			Foy.		Arnaud.
36th Line.	2nd Leger.	4th Leger.	17th Leger, 70th Line.	47th [] [] [] 3 Regts	
[]	[]	[]	[] []	in reserve.	
[]	[]	[]	[] []	31st Leger, 4 Regts.	
[]	[]	[]	[] []	[] []	
[]	[]	2nd Brigade.	[]	▆▆▆▆ ▬	
1st Brigade.					

Sarrut defeated by Wallace, 88th and 45th Regts.

Graindorge defeated by Picton with 8th Portuguese (Major Birmingham).

Foy beaten by Leith. 9th, 38th, and 1st Royals, assisted by 74th Regt. and 8th Portuguese under Colonel Douglas; but 9th did most of this work.

Arnaud defeated on Pass road by 74th Regt. and 21st Portuguese, and Portuguese Artillery under Major von Arentschildt.

Attack on Picton's Third Division.

Order of Events.

(1) September 26th. *Evening.* After sunset Picton sends 88th Regiment to intermediate position between the Pass and Lightburne.

(2) September 27th. *Before daybreak.* On Mackinnon's report of the French assembling in the ravine below the 88th Regiment, Picton sends 4 companies 45th, Major Gwynne, to reinforce 88th Regiment.

(3) Merle's two columns ascend the easy gradient below the 88th Regiment, but turn to their left on coming under artillery fire.

(4) The French light troops gain possession of the Rocks A, and thus cover the right flank of Merle's column—which is making for a position to the French left of those rocks—say

about the rocky point B, of which their *tirailleurs* also get possession—driving out the light companies of the 45th and 88th Regiments from the rocky ridge near there running towards the rocky point C.

(5) *About 6 a.m.* 31st Leger, under Arnaud, attack by Pass road.

(6) Light troops, under Col. Williams, retire to flank of 31st Leger.

(7) Three companies 74th on left of 21st Portuguese and guns prevent 31st Leger from *deploying*.

(8) Picton hands over Pass to Mackinnon and goes to his left.

(9) 8th Portuguese, left wing (Major Birmingham), and 5 companies, 45th (Col. Meade), ordered to follow Picton.

(10) Picton rallies light companies of 45th and 88th Regiments, and Smyth leads them against rocky point B, or perhaps C, of which he gets possession, but is himself killed.

(11) Waller meantime having seen the French drive back light companies, had hurried off for Leith; rides 2 miles and meets Barnes' Brigade, and hurries them on.

(12) 88th Regiment comes to assistance of 45th Regiment (Gwynne) and 3 companies 88th attack rocks A and remainder pass between rocks A and B to the attack of French regiments beginning to deploy on the sloping ground to the east of the line of rocks.

(13) Picton brings 8th Portuguese, left wing (Birmingham), forward immediately afterwards to the attack of French to right of rocks B.

(14) 45th, 4 companies (Gwynne), 88th Regiment (Wallace), and 8th Portuguese, left wing (Birmingham), drive the two French columns, *i.e.* the 36th Line and 2nd and 4th Leger, under Sarrut and Graindorge, down the hill and pursue them to the bottom, the latter general being killed.

(15) While this is going on 3 companies of the 88th Regiment have a fierce struggle for possession of rocks A with 200 French *tirailleurs,* and kill or drive them out.

(16) The 4 companies, 45th (Gwynne), and 88th Regiment (Wallace) begin to return to the neighbourhood of rocks A to re-form, and are too far to the English left to take further part in the battle with Foy now about to begin and from which a cross ridge divides them; the 8th Portuguese (Birmingham) returning to the English right of rocks B.

Battle of Bussaco

(17) When Regnier sees the defeat of Merle's Division he hurries off with anger to Foy, and orders him to attack at once.

(18) Foy, with 7 battalions, 17th Leger and 70th Line, impetuously mount the hill, in 2 columns close together.

(19) Col. Douglas, 8th Portuguese, right wing, having been moved by Leith to left of Pass, fire several volleys at Foy's troops from a flanking position, and the latter finding themselves opposed disengage and form 2 columns, one of which is thus marching diagonally towards the line of retirement of the 8th Portuguese (Major Birmingham), left wing, who, in the climb uphill, become disordered by the bad ground and probably arrive at the crest out of breath, as they would hurry on, seeing the French columns on their left making a fresh attack. They oppose Foy's troops and are obliged to retire. Birmingham has his horse killed, and is on foot when he meets Leith. One of Foy's columns having turned to its left to threaten the Pass, Spry's Brigade is formed to oppose it on the English right of the Pass. This column then again turns and follows Foy, whom they see gaining the crest.

(20) Foy's columns press on and gain the crest, which their *tirailleurs* overrun and gain possession of the rocky ridge, near the Windmill, driving away the 9th Regiment (Portuguese), under Col. Sutton, which was also retiring in disorder when Leith arrived on the scene.

(21) Leith comes on with his British Brigade, and marches past the Pass along the lower road until he gets into a suitable position for advancing in line on the French. The 9th form line and sweep the rocks and then attack the columns of Foy as they attempt to deploy on the east side of the plateau.

38th are close behind 9th, but on one side and 1st Regiment support. The 74th Highlanders and 8th Portuguese (Douglas) assist afterwards with their fire.

(22) Foy is wounded, and all his troops dispersed.

(A) MERLE'S ATTACK.

There are many difficult points in connection with the attacks on the Pass and on the English left of it; but there seems no reason to doubt the general correctness of Gen. Picton's account of what took place at the Pass itself, and during the attacks made by Gen. Merle on Picton's left. The real dispute seems to have arisen from Picton not

BATTLE OF BUSSACO

having seen Foy's last attack, during which also the pressure on the Pass itself was renewed.

Gen. Picton states that the 5th and 83rd Regiments, under Lightburne, were detached to his left, and did not act under his orders. The fact is Wellington himself had this brigade of Lightburne's moved up on to the edge of the high plateau, his idea being (according to Sir John Burgoyne) that if he could keep the great commanding heights, the enemy's gaining the dips in a narrow-edged mountain would not do him any good.

Gen. Picton says he occupied the Pass itself with Col. Mackinnon's Brigade, consisting of the 45th, 74th, and 88th Regiments, amounting to about 1,300 rank and file, and with the 9th and 21st Regiments of Portuguese Infantry, under Col. de Champalimaud, the whole about 3,000 men.

Note.

His division numbered	4,743
Deduct Lightburne's Brigade, including 3 companies 5/90th	1,160
	3,583

Besides the Artillery.

As there were no troops between Picton and Lightburne (a space of about a mile), after sunset on the evening of the 26th, Picton detached the 88th Regiment, under Col. Wallace, to his left to take up an intermediate position about three-quarters of a mile from the Pass, so as to keep up communications between the Pass and the high plateau.

This was done after sunset, in order that the enemy might not perceive it.

Col. Mackinnon having visited the 88th before daybreak on the 27th, was informed that the enemy was collecting in the ravine opposite that regiment, on hearing which, Picton detached, to Col. Wallace's support, 4 companies of the 45th Regiment, under Major Gwynne.

A few minutes after, when the day began to clear up, a smart firing of musketry was heard on the left, apparently proceeding, Picton says, from the point where the 88th had been stationed. It was probably the first contact between the French *tirailleurs* and the light companies of the 45th, 74th, and 88th Regiments, which were driven in by the fire of the *tirailleurs*, who were strong in number and preceded Merle's

PORTUGUESE *CAÇADORE*

FRENCH TIRAILLEUR AND VOLTIGEUR

Division. The whole advance of Merle's column was made from some distance to the French right of the Venda de San Antonio, under the guidance of Capt. Charlet (*aide-de-camp* of Gen. Regnier), who had explored the terrain the evening before. He would then perhaps have observed the absence of troops from that part of the line, afterwards to some extent remedied by Picton.

As Merle's column ascended the rising ground from the ravine it was fired into (it is stated by Capt. Lane, R.A.) at about seventy yards distance by two of Thompson's guns, which had been ordered by Wellington to take up a position on a knoll which jutted out slightly to the front, below and to the south of the high plateau.

Some of the 36th Regiment of the Line belonging to Gen. Sarrut's Brigade came close up to these guns, one man being killed eight paces from them. The gunners gave three cheers and saluted the immense column with a few rounds of case and round-shot together, which drove them more to their left, and added to the confusion already existing in their ranks, due to the roughness of the ground, which was strewn with stones amongst the heather.

In the meantime, opposite the Pass, fourteen of the enemy's guns posted on knolls there to the French left of the village of S. Antonio do Cantaro had opened a violent cannonade on the troops and guns stationed at the Pass, while the 31st Leger (4 regiments) drove in the advanced pickets of the division with great impetuosity, and endeavoured to push up the road and force the Pass.

The light corps of the division, unable to resist such a superiority of numbers in front, was most judiciously withdrawn to the flank of the advancing column by Lt.-Col. Williams, and the 31st Leger was received with so steady and well-directed fire by the 21st Portuguese Line Regiment and 3 companies of the 74th Regiment that moved up to their support on the left, that after a long struggle and repeated desperate attempts to deploy into line before advancing further up the hill (during which they suffered much also from the well-directed fire of the Portuguese Artillery, under Major Von Arentschildt), they had to desist; but the enemy still kept up their firing of musketry and round-shot on the Pass, and succeeded in dismounting two Portuguese guns by the use of a heavy battery; but a Portuguese shell having shortly afterwards set fire to the ammunition tumbril, which blew up, the French abandoned the battery.

About this period the firing on the left appearing to increase, and draw nearer, and being satisfied that the 31st Leger could make no

Major-General Leith

serious impression on the troops in position at the Pass, Gen. Picton handed over charge of them to Col. Mackinnon, and rode off with the assistant adjutant-general, Major Pakenham, leaving his *aide-de-camp*, Capt. Cuthbert, and the assistant quartermaster-general, Capt. Anderson, to bring along to the left one battalion of the 8th Portuguese Regiment, under Major Birmingham, and the five remaining companies of the 45th Regiment, under Col. Meade.

On reaching the high rocky point, probably C, about half-way between the Pass of S. Antonio and the high plateau, Gen. Picton found the light companies of the 74th and 88th Regiments outnumbered and "retiring in disorder," and the head of the enemy's column already in possession of a strong rocky point (B or C), deliberately firing down on the Allied troops, and the remainder of a large column pushing up the hill with great rapidity. Whilst endeavouring to rally the light infantry companies, with the assistance of Major Pakenham, he was joined by Major Smyth, of the 45th Regiment, and these officers succeeded in forming them under the immediate fire of the enemy, not more than sixty yards distant. Major Smyth most gallantly led them to the charge, and gained possession of the rocks, driving the enemy before him; but he fell in the moment of victory, which was chiefly due to his animating example.

Before continuing the description of these French attacks, it must be mentioned that there were several groups of rocks standing out above the other rocks round them, some of which were at various times occupied by the heads of French columns or by *tirailleurs*. We will call them A, B, C, D, and E. We have just detailed the account of the French being driven by the light companies of the 45th and 88th Regiments, under Major Smyth, from the group of rocks which we call C, but the rocks may have been B. Shortly we shall read of the French being driven out of the left group (or A) rocks by 3 companies of the 88th Regiment, under Capts. Dunne, Dansey, and Oates. Further to the English right (close to the Pass) was the group of rocks called D, occupied by the 74th Regiment throughout the day. From the Pass of S. Antonio do Cantaro to the rocky point A, the rocks are continuous, except for a short space to the English left of Leith's Windmill, and on the right of the Pass was much higher rocky ground called E.

We must now return to Merle's column, which had been turned to its left by the fire of Thompson's two guns. This brought it to the English right of the original position occupied by the 88th Regiment, and the 4 companies of the 45th, under Major Gwynne, which were at this time on the right of and in front of the 88th Regiment; while further to the right still were the light companies, which after being driven back in some disorder had been rallied by Gen. Picton, Major Pakenham, and Major Smyth, and were about to advance under the latter's gallant leading against the French ensconced in rocks near C.

Picton's narrative continues:

> The Assistant Q.M. General having fortunately brought up a battalion of the 8th Portuguese Regt. commanded by Major Birmingham, at this critical period, I personally led and directed their attack on the flank of the enemy's column, and we completely succeeded in driving them in great confusion and disorder down the hill and across the ravine. (I believe this to have been Graindorge's column, *i.e.* the 4th Regiment.)

It will be observed that Picton says nothing here about the 88th and half 45th Regiment. This is because the 8th Portuguese probably attacked Graindorge's regiment, the 4th Leger, whose screen of *tirailleurs* were probably the troops just repulsed from C rocks by the light companies. It is probable also that the smoke and fog prevented him from seeing very far and a ridge also intervened between him and the 88th Regiment. I assume that at this time further on Picton's left the 88th and half 45th were attacking the 36th and 2nd Leger, under Sarrut, and this an 88th subaltern describes as follows:

> From the cloud of sharpshooters who crowned the heights immediately in front of the 88th Regt. Colonel Wallace thought himself menaced by a dense body, and was in the act of telling his men the mode of attack he intended to adopt, when Captain Dunne, who had been sent by the colonel to see what was going on on his right (for there was a heavy fog), returned with information that some 100 of the enemy's troops occupied a cluster of rocks close beside him (which I take to be A rocks), and that a column was moving on the open ground between the 3rd and 5th Divisions, and as these rocks formed a pivot for their operations, the colonel formed a resolution of changing his front, storming the rocks, and attacking the column.
> (*N.B.*—I take it that he had before been facing nearly east and that he proceeded to the south in column, forming line facing north-east when he arrived at the scene of action.)
> At this time the 45th were engaged with numbers out of pro-

portion, but they gallantly maintained their ground. The 5th, 74th, and 83rd were likewise attacked; but the 88th from the nature of their situation came in contact with the full body of the enemy, and while opposed to 3 times their number were assailed on their *left* by a couple of hundred riflemen stationed on the rocks A.

Colonel Wallace had scarcely reached the rocks when a fire as destructive as it was animated, assailed him.

The moment was a critical one, but he never lost his presence of mind. He ordered his 2 front companies to attack the rocks and another to turn them, while he pressed forward with the remainder of his regiment against the main body.

The 8th Portuguese were close on the enemy, and opened a well-directed fire while the 45th were performing prodigies of valour.

(Note.—All the 88th Regiment did not consider it well directed.)

At this moment the 88th came up to the assistance of their comrades and the 3 regiments (45th and 88th British and 8th Portuguese, Birmingham) charged. A terrific contest took place, the French fought well, but they had no chance with our men when we grappled close with them, and they were overthrown, leaving half of their column on the heather with which the hill was covered.

While the 88th and 45th and 8th Portuguese were thus engaged the 2 companies (really 3) had a severe struggle with the riflemen on the rocks A. The French ranged amphitheatrically one above the other, took a murderous aim at our soldiers in their advance to dislodge them, officers as well as privates became personally engaged in a hand to hand fight. Captain Dunne fought with his sabre, while Captain Dansey made use of a firelock and bayonet; he received 3 wounds, and Captain Dunne owed his life to a serjeant of his company named Brazill, who, seeing his officer in danger of being overpowered, scrambled to his assistance, and making a thrust of his halbert at the Frenchman, transfixed him against the rock he was standing on. (Halberts such as the sergeants carried can be seen at the Royal United Service Institute.)

A contest of this sort could not possibly be of long duration, but it was nevertheless of a very serious kind. The enemy were numerous, well disciplined, and full of ardour, and besides, from the nature of their position, they had but the alternative of driving our men down, or being themselves flung from the crags amongst which they fought. The latter was the result; for although they combated with a defensive suited to the situation in which they were placed, the heroes of Austerlitz, Essling, and Wagram were hurled from the rocks by the Rangers of Connaught.

The defeat of Merle's Division is not surprising, if we bear in mind the statement of the French writers on the subject.

The columns arrived out of breath at the crest of the plateau, and in disorder from the bad ground they had traversed; they tried to deploy under cover of their *tirailleurs*; but the head of each column was caught by the Allies in the midst of the movement, and their destruction by the latter, who had previously deployed into line, and who were acting now on the French front and flank, was inevitable.

The fire of a line is terrific in comparison with that of a column, and to the French were added the disadvantages of being out of breath, on lower sloping ground, and of being in a state of disorder.

When therefore the first fire was delivered by the Allies and the charge with fixed bayonets was made, all was practically over.

It was the same at Vimiero, and in this battle on three occasions:

Craufurd's charge,

Merle's defeat,

Foy's defeat, also in subsequent Peninsular battles, and so late as at Waterloo.

(B) FOY'S ATTACK.

Immediately Regnier saw the repulse of Merle's Division take place he rode up to Gen. Foy, who was supporting Arnaud in his attack along the Pass road, and angrily called out to him:

"*Pourquoi ne montez-vous pas? On fait marcher les troupes quand on veut. Vous ne faites rien.*"

Foy says he had not the presence of mind to answer, but he ordered "the charge" to be beaten; ordered the 70th to follow *en masse* and to his left—put himself at the head of the 17th and climbed the mountain—"seeking death rather than victory."

They climbed under a terrible fire, their masses "receiving all and giving nothing."

At two-thirds of the distance they were fired into by the 8th Por-

PENDURADA.

Taken from a bare knoll on its south-east, which was the site of a French battery attacking the Pass.

View looking north from E High Rocks on right of S. Antonio do Cantaro
Pass looking along the ridge towards the higher Serra da Bussaco occupied by
Lightburne's Division, and Spencer's Division further on. Foy gained the crest
near the nearest windmill in the picture. Merle came up further north in the centre
of the picture.

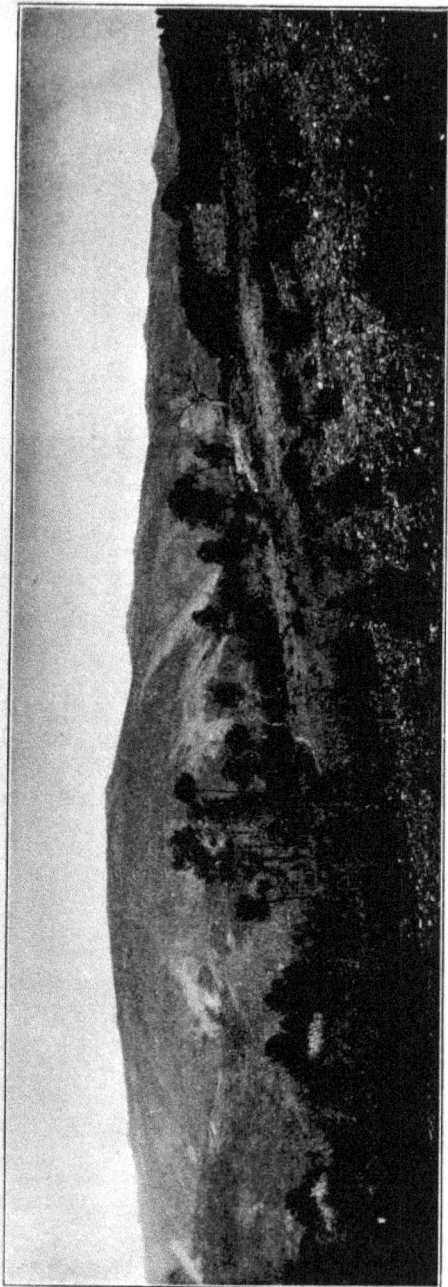

View of Allied right from nearly extreme French left.

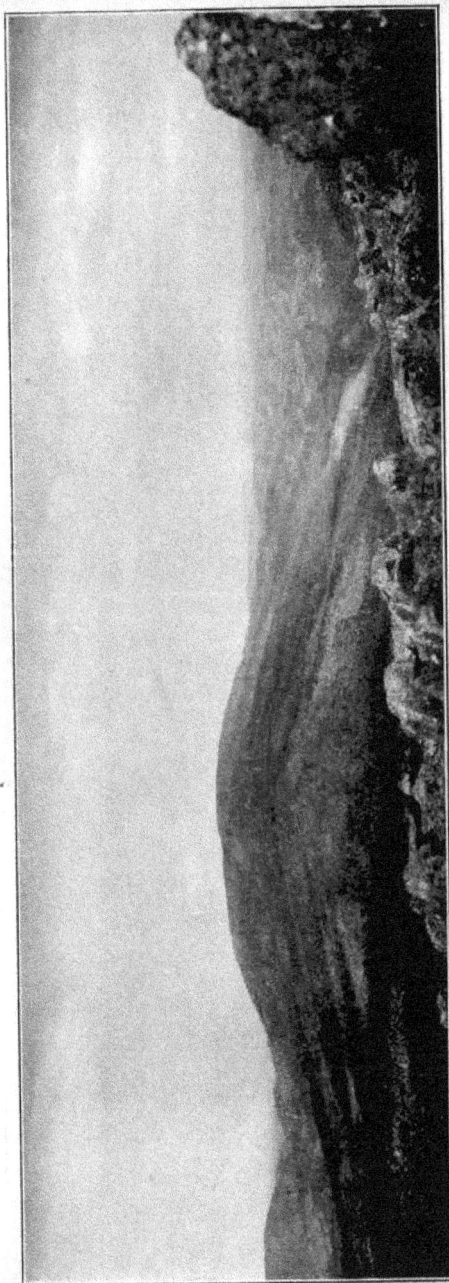

From high rocks E on English right of S. Antonio do Cantaro Pass, looking across Pass, northwards, to Leith's Windmill at Little Pass, past rocky points A, B, C to 2-gun knoll and high Serra (Spencer's position).

On the right Foy's attack and further on Merle's attack.

From high rocks E on English right of S. Antonio do Cantaro Pass, looking across Pass, northwards, to Leith's Windmill at Little Pass, past rocky points A, B, C to 2-gun knoll and high Serra (Spencer's position).

On the right Foy's attack and further on Merle's attack.

2-gun knoll, taken from the False Pass side, occupied by 88th Connaught Rangers on 26th September, 1810.

FRENCH SIDE.

From a stone cross near the bottom of the valley looking up at D rocks on the sky-line at the right of the S. Antonio do Cantaro Pass. The Pass road is seen at the extreme left of the picture as it passes the break in the rocky ridge.

Pass. D Rocky Point. Leith's Windmill.

FRENCH SIDE.

The S. Antonio do Cantaro Pass road, taken from the extreme left
of the French position.

FRENCH SIDE.

D rocks.

E rocks.

The Pass of S. Antonio do Cantaro where it crosses at the highest point of the road. Taken from the Allied rear.

The right of the S. Antonio do Cantaro Pass, near the top, occupied by the 21st Portuguese under Champalimaud.

FRENCH SIDE.

The scene of Foy's defeat by Leith.

Slope, taken from the ridge to (Allied) left of Foy's attack, looking north. The ridge here hid the scene of Foy's defeat from those to the northward.

ALLIED SIDE.

The Windmill Pass, to (Allied) left of Leith's Windmill, the scene of Foy's defeat as he tried to deploy. It was hidden from those engaged just before in the fight between Wallace and Merle, there being a rocky shoulder intervening. A cartroad (and foot-path) still go through this little pass, the former being shown in Wyld's map. In the centre is seen the road from S. Antonio to Moira.

tuguese (Col. Douglas), Foy's horse was shot, and he mounted that of his *aide-de-camp*, which also was struck by two bullets at the top of the mountain, but it had the glory of being the only French horse that reached the top of the Alcoba on that day. Foy's column, on receiving the fire of the 8th Portuguese (Douglas) on their left flank, broke into two columns and made to their right, and although the 70th went temporarily to its left, it soon turned back and followed Foy.

On arriving at the crest, the plateau was found covered with the Allied troops.

Those on our left made a movement and we were overwhelmed with battalion fire, upon our front the enemy hidden behind rocks assassinated us with impunity: the head of my column was thrown, in spite of me, to the right, I could not succeed in deploying, and disorder ensued. The 17th and 70th took to flight, vying who could do it best.

(*i.e.* on their left the 8th Portuguese, under Douglas, and possibly half the 45th Regiment, under Col. Meade; upon their front the 9th Regiment—British).

Foy was then wounded in the arm, and carried away by his soldiers, in their flight, down to the bottom of the hill.

Sarrut, with 4 regiments, is said by Koch to have accompanied Foy in this attack; but his aid, if given, was not efficacious.

The English accounts of Foy's attack are rather confusing, but careful study points to the following as being the truth about the matter.

The 88th, 4 companies of the 45th, and the 8th Portuguese, under Birmingham, followed the defeated troops of Merle a good way down the mountain, and it would take them a considerable time to recover their former position.

Now we must bear in mind that the 8th Portuguese (Birmingham) were on the English right of the victorious attack on Merle, and therefore would probably return up the hill nearly in the same relative position, which would be near the scene of Foy's attack, at this time distinctly in progress. The battalion was now under Major Birmingham's control, as Picton had gone back to the Pass apparently without giving any fresh orders as to what was to be done on the left of the Pass.

As Foy came along, he says he was attacked on the left flank by a battalion which was almost certainly the 8th Portuguese, under Col. Douglas, who says:

We had not moved fifty paces before we found ourselves engaged with a French column moving up the hill, who finding
themselves opposed in front and seeing an unoccupied inter-
val on our left, discontinued their attack on us and by a flank
movement gained the crest of the position on the left. Here
they had not had time to dress their platoons before they were
charged by Sir James Leith at the head of a British Brigade, of
which the 9th was the regiment nearest to me. In this charge
we joined by an oblique movement, etc. I was in communication with the C.O. of the Royal Scots during our advance.

From Col. Douglas's testimony I think it is evident that this battalion of the 8th Portuguese behaved well. He goes so far as to say that
Wellington rode up as they were returning from the charge, shook
hands with him, and did more than justice to the regiment.

General Leith's account of his movements is very fully given in his
letter of the 10th November, 1810, to Lord Wellington. They may be
summarised as follows:

Finding no attack was being made on his right or front, in accordance with orders, he moved soon after daybreak to his left, to support
Picton.

Leith rode to the Pass in advance of his troops to see what was
going on.

Major V. Arentschildt's guns at the Pass being short of ammunition,
Leith ordered his divisional battery of four 6-pounders to be placed
there, which was done. Two of Leith's guns had remained at the redoubt of the Chapel of N.S. de Monte Alto, and joined Gen. Hill's
Corps in the retreat from Bussaco.

Leith found Col. Douglas with one battalion 8th Portuguese and
Brig.-Gen. Spry's Brigade in line in front of the rocky ridge near Arentschildt's guns. (Spry's Line Regiments: 3rd Portuguese, 2 battalions,
15th Portuguese, 2 battalions.) This fixes Douglas's position before he
moved the fifty yards of which he writes and fixes the first direction
of Foy's attack. The 9th Portuguese Regiment (Col. Sutton) was also
in line at the Pass. Leith ordered Col. Douglas with his right battalion,
8th Portuguese, to move to his left to support the point attacked.

He also ordered the 9th Portuguese (Col. Sutton) to move to the
support of Picton's position, *i.e.* to the left of Pass, also Spry's Brigade
was ordered to its left to remain in reserve *at the Pass.* Leith says:

The enemy during this movement disengaged part of his leading column and branched into two, the first continuing to its right, the head of the second pointing towards its left and threatening the position on the right of the road from S. Antonio do Cantaro, which caused Spry's Brigade to be formed; this column, however, when the first column had succeeded, turned towards its right also, and followed the other, which was gaining the ascent of the Sierra; the enemy was still advancing, and had every appearance of succeeding in forcing that part of Major-Gen. Picton's position which is on the left of the road of S. Antonio do Cantaro, *where several rocky eminences crown the ridge of the Sierra.*

Foy's troops on gaining the crest attacked with their fire the *left* battalion of the 8th Portuguese, under Major Birmingham; and the 9th Regiment, Portuguese, under Col. Sutton, which (says Leith) having been severely pressed had given way, and "were rapidly retiring in complete confusion and disorder." Other witnesses also testify to this fact. Major Birmingham was on foot, his horse having been killed, and he gave this information to Gen. Leith, who succeeded in stopping the retiring troops.

It may be here remarked that Picton (in his letter to Wellington, 10th November, 1810) states that the 5 companies of the 45th Regiment, under Col. Meade, and the 8th Portuguese, right wing, under Col. Douglas, were concerned in repulsing the last (Foy's) attempt of the enemy. This is important, as Col. Meade and his 5 companies of the 45th Regiment are missing from all accounts, from the time they were sent to repulse Merle's attack along with Major Birmingham's *left* wing of the 8th Portuguese. They left with Birmingham, but did not join in under Picton in repulsing Merle. At any rate, no published account says so.

Leith having joined his British Brigade on the reverse slope of the Sierra took it up the slope near the Windmill, formed the 9th British Regiment in line, ordered the 38th to follow in support, and the 1st Royals to act as reserve. The 9th attacked the French at the rocky ridge and drove the whole down the hill with the bayonet, with the 38th close behind them, *i.e.* Leith with 1 regiment defeated Foy's 7 regiments of the 17th Leger and 70th Line, who had been unable to deploy in time.

This seems to have been a notable exploit, and the greatest loss Foy's troops sustained seems to have been owing to the destructive fire of the 9th British Regiment poured in after their bayonet charge; their fire being supplemented by that of the 74th Highlanders, who advanced on their right.

A curious point here is that the officers of Barnes' British Brigade saw nothing of Meade's 5 companies of the 45th during this operation, but I think they must have been ensconced in the rocks between the Windmill and the Pass.

A perusal of Capt. Gomm's letter of 1st November, 1810, to Major Gomm, also Sir John Cameron's letters to Col. Napier of 9th and 21st August, 1834, and 21st November, 1835, Col. Waller's Memorandum, Col. Taylor's of 26th April, 1832, to Col. Napier, is recommended to the reader, all of which will be found in the Appendix.

I would also refer to my plans, showing the position of affairs at various stages of the attacks on Picton's position, which, I trust, will be found to agree with the authentic accounts of what took place. I trust also that the photographs of the terrain will assist the reader.

Professor Oman's account.

Although admiring the assiduity with which the various phases of Merle's and Foy's attacks have been investigated by Prof. Oman, I find myself unfortunately in disagreement with him on the following points:—

Vol. III.—states that Picton detached first a wing of the 45th, under Major Gwynne, and then the two battalions of the 8th Portuguese to fill the unoccupied space which intervened between him and the 88th. It is clear Picton sent only the *left* battalion of the 8th Portuguese under Major Birmingham. The mistake is repeated on the next page:

Major Smyth's attack on the rocks B or C, with the rallied light company of the 45th and 88th, took place *prior* to the charge of the 3 regiments on the French. Smyth's men charged and obtained possession of the rocks B or C, and he was himself killed. Perhaps Prof. Oman has some authority (unpublished) for his statement that they afterwards took part in the repulse of Sarrut or Graindorge, which is, of course, likely, but I know of none.

Prof. Oman here gives no credit to the 8th Portuguese (left wing) under Picton, who attacked, I think, Graindorge's column, the 4th Leger.

The British regiments, 88th and 45th, are said to have descended to the bottom of the hill in pursuit, and then to have returned to their former position, thus missing Foy's attack, "which occurred just along

94

the hillside just to the *left* of the point at which their collision with Merle's battalions had taken place," according to Prof. Oman.

I think it is clear that Foy's attack took place to the right (English) of where Merle was defeated, otherwise Foy *must* have crossed the line of retirement of the 88th and 45th. On the same page the Professor states that Foy "chose as his objective the first and lowest hill-top to the French right of the Pass of San Antonio."

This admits that the point attacked was considerably to the right (English) of the place where Merle was defeated; but I think Foy's troops arrived on the crest near the Windmill by the branch road which comes up near there (*vide* plans).

The troops which were in front of Foy were:

Right wing of 45th, under Colonel Meade.

Portuguese 8th of the Line, which had just been aiding in the repulse of Merle.

It was the left wing only of the 8th Portuguese which aided in the repulse of Merle, and Leith confirms their dispersal by Foy, but the Professor misses the point that the right wing of the 8th Portuguese, under Douglas, was at this time operating on Foy's left flank.

These were soon afterwards joined by 1 battalion of the 9th Portuguese from Champalimaud's Brigade and the unattached battalion of the Thomar Militia, which Picton sent up the hill.

I think we should here read *Leith* for *Picton* (*vide* the former's statement in letter to Wellington and *vide* Prof. Oman's note). Wellington, Napier, and Oman spell Col. Champalimaud's name wrongly as Champelmond.

At the moment when Foy's attack was beginning, Leith had just reached the Pass of S. Antonio with various troops.

Leith says he galloped *ahead* of his troops to the Pass.

One of Dickson's Portuguese Batteries was also with him.

Leith calls them "the 6-pounder brigade of his Corps," which he says "moved with the British Brigade." Major Dickson says that he only succeeded in getting two of his guns to the Pass.

Napier and Oman both say that the 38th Regiment was sent on to get between the enemy and the reverse slope of the position, or to turn the enemy's flank, but that the 38th was unable to climb what

Napier calls a precipice, and Oman a steep thickly covered with boulders; and Oman says it came back.

Leith, however, only says he "*intended* the 38th to move on in rear and to the left of the 9th Regiment, to have turned the enemy beyond the rocky eminence."

Leith changed his mind, and "the 38th were therefore directed to form also and support," which they did at a short distance, and actually assisted, according to Capt. Gomm, in the attack on Foy's troops, being on the right of the 9th Regiment. In the turning movement which Napier and Oman speak of as having taken place, they would have been a good deal to the left of the 9th, and would have been too late to take any part in the attack.

Professor Oman's Plan of Regnier's attack.

A careful study of all the evidence available convinces me that the positions on this plan are incorrect, as follows:—

(1) Wellington's position, and that of Thompson's 2 guns, is too far to the left and too far to the front.

(2) The positions of the 88th and half 45th Regiments are nearly those occupied by the 88th on the 26th September, and not their positions at the time of Merle's repulse. They should be shown 700 to 800 metres more to the right.

(3) The 2 battalions of the 8th Portuguese are shown wrongly. One battalion (Birmingham's) should be 400 to 500 metres more to the right, and the other (Douglas's) 700 metres more to the right. They were never together in the fight.

(4) Merle is shown as attacking in 3 columns, whereas he had only 2, and he attacked 500 metres to the English right of the point indicated on the plan.

Note Regarding the Position of the Village of S. Antonio Do Cantaro.

Gen. Koch, in *Memoirs de Masséna*, says: General Merle was ordered to form his division at the foot of the mountain, to the right of the Venda de S. Antonio.

General Foy with the 1st Brigade of the division Heudelet was to occupy S. Antonio, by the 31st Leger, and to keep the other regiment of his Brigade in rear of this village. Gen. Heudelet, with the 2nd Brigade and the Light Cavalry, were also ordered to be behind the same village.

THE CHURCH AND VILLAGE OF S. ANTONIO DÓ CANTARO.

Baron Fririon. The division Merle assembled before daylight at the foot of the Serra de S. Antonio do Cantaro; the 31st Leger were at the Venda de S. Antonio supported by Foy.

The modern map shows the village of S. Antonio do Cantaro as on the main road; but so-called guides show strangers a village much to the French right of the main road as being the village of above name. It is connected by a fair road with the main road, and Wyld's map shows a village in this position off the road. An old Government map in the British Museum shows the village as being on the main road.

The advance of Merle's column took place nearly opposite the village shown on the modern map as Pendurada.

Note as to Colonel Meade's Half-Battalion, 45th Regiment.

Prof. Oman, Vol. 1, page 372, says that "the leading regiment of Merle's column was lurching over the skyline on to the little plateau above just as the defenders arrived. The 88th descending from the British left, the wing of the 45th and the 2 battalions of the 8th Portuguese coming along the hill road from the right. Col. Wallace of the 88th threw out 3 of his companies to cover his flanks, called to the wing of the 45th to fall in on his right, and charged the flank of Merle's disordered mass.

At the same moment the 8th Portuguese a little further along the hill-top deployed and opened a rolling fire against the front of the enemy, while Wellington came up with 2 of Thompson's guns and turned their fire upon the flank and rear of the climbing mass. Apparently at the same instant the light companies of the 45th and 88th which had been engaged with the French *tirailleurs* and had been driven away far to their right were rallied by Picton in person, and brought up along the plateau to the right of the 8th Portuguese. They drew up only sixty yards from the flank of the leading French regiment, and opened a rolling fire upon it."

With regard to the above description I can only say that I regard it as erroneous.

It appears clear that the 88th Regiment, under Wallace, and Major Gwynne's 4 companies of the 45th Regiment acted together against Merle, and I have no doubt that they attacked Sarrut's column while Picton in charge of a battalion of the 8th Portuguese, under Picton and Major Birmingham, was a little further to the English right attacking Graindorge. If Picton and Wallace were attacking in the same place the same enemy, Picton would not have written to Wellington:

The colonel of the 88th and Major Gwynne of the 45th are entitled to the whole of the credit, and I can claim no merit whatever in the executive part of that brilliant exploit which your Lordship has so justly extolled.

In his despatch, Wellington wrote in general terms and did not go into details, but summarised the matter, and gave credit to the 88th, the 45th, and the 8th Portuguese.

As to Picton: (*a*) He rallied the light companies of the 45th and 88th and sent them against the rocks under Major Smyth, but this fight was all over before the others began, as already stated above, (*b*) He directed the attack of the 8th Portuguese, under Major Birmingham, but he regarded Wallace's exploit as a matter separate from these. I believe, all the same, that as the two attacks on Merle's 2 columns developed, the two allied bodies came near together *on the slope of the hill*.

They were not acting in concert at first, for it is on record that the 8th Portuguese:

> . . . . posted on a rising ground on our right (*i.e.* of the 88th Regiment), and a little in our rear in place of advancing with us, opened a distant and ill-directed fire, and one which would exactly cross the path of the 88th as that corps was moving to meet the French column, which consisted of three splendid regiments. Wallace, seeing the loss and confusion that would infallibly ensue, sent Lieut. John Fitzpatrick, an officer of tried gallantry, with orders to point out to the regiment the error into which it had fallen, but Fitzpatrick had only time to take off his hat and call out, '*Vamos camarados,*' when he received two bullets, one from the Portuguese which passed through his back, and the other in his left leg from the French—yet this regiment continued to fire away regardless of the consequences.

Wallace then charged with the 88th and Gwynne's 4 companies of the 45th, and no doubt the 8th Portuguese, under Major Birmingham, soon found out their mistake and joined in against that part of the French opposite to them, which would be Graindorge's column.

It must be noted that Prof. Oman does not distinguish in his account between the two wings of the 45th British.

It was Major Gwynne's troops who did so well, not Col. Meade's; but Prof. Oman talks of the latter as coming along with the 8th Portuguese, and as being called upon by Wallace to fall in on his right—although Prof. Oman's plan shows the 45th, under Meade, at the Pass,

PORTUGUESE TROOPS REPELLING THE FRENCH ATTACK

and the 2 battalions 8th Portuguese a thousand metres to the English left of the Pass, which cannot be said to bear out the text, which says they came along from the right together. There is little or no evidence of Col. Meade having done anything in the fight, but Major Gwynne was all along with Wallace, and fell severely wounded at his side; and his 4 companies were on the left of the 88th at the time of the charge.

(3) Prof. Oman follows Napier as to Wellington bringing up 2 guns at this juncture, and directing their fire on Merle's column.

Both historians are, I think, mistaken. These 2 guns turned Merle's column earlier in the morning. Capt. Lane says of this artillery division:

> My men did their duty, etc. The French Voltigeurs came close to the guns and one was killed only eight paces off. An immense column showed itself in the ravine—we with three cheers gave them a few rounds of case and round shot together at about seventy paces distance, which drove them back.

It will be seen that these 2 guns were detached, and if any such notable occurrence as that mentioned by Napier and Oman had taken place, Capt. Lane would certainly have referred to it, for he was a ready writer. It would have been necessary to take the guns to the low ground, as they could not see Merle's column from the 2-gun knoll, where they had been previously posted, and where Wyld's map marks them as placed during the whole attack by Merle, while the other 4 guns were with Lightburne higher up.

Sir John Burgoyne also wrote in his *Diary*:

> The enemy's column had been turned in their direction by two guns under Captain Lane, posted under the great height, who received them with some rounds of grape.

As regards the conduct of the various regiments engaged with the enemy on this occasion, praise has been bestowed by Wellington in his despatches on many that well deserved it, but there were others who were overlooked, either because a general commanding on such occasions cannot be everywhere, or often does not receive very full reports from the divisional commanders. The latter, too, are often very much like the general public; they are impressed by a brilliant charge made by some particular regiment which comes under their personal notice, but which is over in a few minutes, while the probably more onerous and meritorious work done by other regiments, but not rendered conspicuous by any such circumstance, is passed over.

At Bussaco, many regiments had to sustain the fire of the enemy's *tirailleurs*, and in some cases of their artillery, without being able to make reply. This is very trying to troops, and in this way the 5th and 83rd Regiments, under Lightburne, suffered a good deal.

There was no adequate force of Allied skirmishers at that point, which at first threatened to be seriously assailed.

The 74th Regiment at the Pass, too, suffered a good deal until they were allowed to attack the enemy opposed to them, which they did most effectively, driving them to the bottom of the mountain.

The burthen of the fight, however, fell most heavily upon the Allied skirmishers. The *Caçadores* distinguished themselves greatly through-out the day. This word means "Hunters," and this kind of fighting suited them as well as their name.

Every division, from those on Craufurd's position to the S. Antonio Pass, had their own skirmishers out to their front in addition to the 60th Rifles, which were broken up and distributed along the line; but Lt.-Col. Williams, who was twice wounded, had a special command, consisting of the 3 light companies, 60th Rifles, and those of the 45th, 88th, 74th, and 90th Regiments, to which reference is made in the Appendix.

In this respect the light companies of the King's German Legion, the 7th and 79th Foot, the 95th Rifles, the 45th, 74th, and 88th Foot all did good service, and most of them got little credit.

Their services in keeping in check the enemy's *tirailleurs*, and in disorganising the attacking columns, could not have been too highly praised.

GENERAL CRAUFURD AT THE BATLE OF BUSSACO

CHAPTER 10

The Attack on the Light Division, Including that on Pack's Division

Masséna ordered Ney with the 6th Corps to attack "by the two roads which lead upon the route of Coimbra" (see note in Masséna's Order for the battle, in Appendix). He was apparently referring to the two roads A and B, both of which were visible from Moura.

He was using a bad map by Lopez, and his other information about the roads was also misleading.

It seems certain that he intended two columns to start from the neighbourhood of Moura by roads A and B, both of which can be traced at present, and are shown in parts by the accompanying illustrations.

Loison would march by A, and Marchand by B.

Loison's Division was to attack, *via* Sula, as soon as the 2nd Corps (Regnier, or Reynier) had appeared on the crest of the mountain, i.e. north of the San Antonio do Cantaro Pass.

Marchand was to support Loison by advancing on his left by road B, and Mermet was to be in reserve.

The 3rd Division of the 6th Corps, Gen. Loison, consisted of:

Simon's Brigade.

26th Ligne (5th, 6th, and 7th Battalions)⎱
Légion du Midi   ..   ..⎰ 6 Battalions.
Légion Hanovrienne (2 Battalions)   ..⎰

Ferey's Brigade.

32nd Leger (2nd Battalion)   ..   ..⎱
66th Ligne (4th, 5th, and 6th Battalions)⎱6 Battalions.
82nd Ligne (4th and 6th Battalions)   ..⎰

(In all, about 6,800 officers and men.)

Porta dá Sulla.

Windmill.

Sula.

Looking from near Moira at the positions of—

SPENCER.   PACK.   COLEMAN.   CRAUFURD.   COLE.

(MARCHAND'S ATTACK.)   (LOISON'S ATTACK.)

(Shows road he took.)

CRAUFURD'S WINDMILL FROM THE ALLIED REAR.

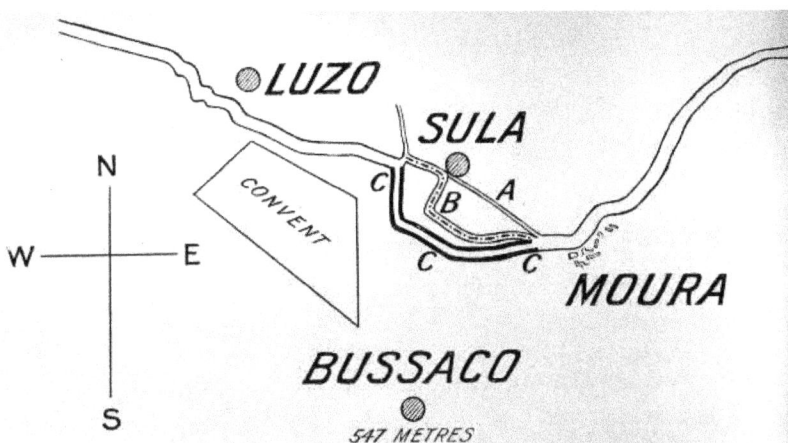

On referring to Plan it will be seen that from near Moira, or Moura, three roads branch off in a direction generally westerly.

A is the direct road from Moira to Sula, or Sulla. It is marked on an old War Office map to be seen in the British Museum.

B is the road as marked on Wyld's maps, which are from the Official Survey by Sir William Mitchell.

C C is the modern road. It did not exist between the points C and C at the time of the battle. Unless care be taken, it is easy to fall into the error of supposing that B and C C are the same road. It looks as though Prof. Oman has made this mistake.

The 1st Division of the 6th Corps, Gen. Marchand, consisted of—

Maucune's Brigade.

6th Leger (1st and 2nd Battalions)
69th Ligne (1st, 2nd, and 3rd Battalions) } 5 Battalions.
(Who fought at Marengo.)

Marcognet's Brigade.

39th Ligne (1st, 2nd, and 3rd Battalions) } 6 Battalions.
76th Ligne (1st, 2nd, and 3rd Battalions)

(In all, about 6,600 officers and men.)

The total force about to attack in the neighbourhood of Sulla numbered, therefore, about 13,400 in 23 battalions.

The above two divisions had as their reserve the 2nd Division of the 6th Corps, under Gen. Mermet, in number about 7,600.

Fririon, chief of Masséna's Staff, gave the numbers as:

Gen. Loison	6916
Gen. Marchand	6658
	13574
Gen. Mermet	7023
	20597

Loison's Division was disposed in mass by brigades, and was preceded by the usual skirmishing line, which was engaged very early before the actual attack; and was furnished probably almost entirely by other corps, in accordance with the French custom.

After Regnier's troops appeared on the crest to the French right of the San Antonio Pass, Loison commenced his advance, *i.e.* about 7 a.m. He soon began to encounter serious opposition from large numbers of Anglo-Portuguese skirmishers below the village of Sula, but a statement made that the village itself had been prepared for defence is not correct. It is said, however, that the French *tirailleurs* had to be strongly reinforced before the front could be cleared and the village got possession of. One account says this took three-quarters of an hour, which is unlikely.

What actually took place at this village has not been carefully recorded anywhere, but there is reason to believe that the opposition was such as to make it necessary to detach troops round the flanks of the defence before the Allied light troops could be induced to retire; and it may here be noted that any troops which found themselves on the left of the village would come across two roads which apparently led towards the Sulla Gate of the convent enclosure, and there is some evidence that one battalion of Ferey's Division followed one of these roads and passed to the French left of the Light Division.

Craufurd had in his skirmishing line:

95th Rifles	766
3rd Caçadores	656
Riflemen, K.G.L. (probably)	90
	1512

When these light troops were driven out of Sula, either by a turning movement or by superior numbers, they retired up the abutment

Craufurd's position from the French point of view.

Craufurd's rock is on the sky-line at top centre, and the wall of rock extends from it to the road on the extreme right, which road is not however visible.

of the mountain, loading and firing, and were at this time (according to Prof. Oman) reinforced by the 1st Caçadores, 546 officers and men; so that, if this is correct, the advancing French column had to contend with some 2,000 skirmishers, principally on their left flank, who could not well retire otherwise than to that side, owing to the deep gully on the right of the French, and the fire of the guns above. Both sides would have difficulty in using the actual road, as the Engineers had broken up all the roads by which attacks could be made.

The space available on the tongue of land for the French advance was only about 130 yards broad (at 50 yards distance below the Windmill, or 30 yards from the crest), the Windmill being on higher ground 20 yards above the crest.

There is a trench running the whole length of the crest defended by Craufurd, probably made by him. (But possibly by the Portuguese in the Army Manoeuvres of a few years ago. It may have been made by road-makers requiring metal.) Of the above 130 yards, 50 yards on the French right, *i.e.* from the road to the left, was blocked by a steep wall of rock, 10 or 12 feet high, quite impassable by a heavily laden soldier.

As the French advanced up the face of the hill, on their left of the road, a more or less direct fire from Ross's and part, or all, Bull's Horse Artillery, in all, 12 guns, 6-pounders, and a flank fire from the light troops, had now to be endured by the column for eight or ten minutes, while the steep face of the hill was ascended; but of the guns, only Bull's could see the column when once on the steep, until they neared the crest. This threw them into some disorder, but the advance was most gallantly continued in the space between Ross's guns and the road. We are told by French accounts that their objective was now these guns, of which they obtained temporary possession of three, but the English accounts say the guns were all withdrawn, which one French historian confirms.

★★★★★★

Napier says: "The edge of the tableland on which the Light Division stood was very abrupt, and formed a salient angle, behind the apex of which the 43rd and 52nd were drawn up in line, the right of the one and the left of the other resting on the very edges; the artillery was at the apex, looking down the descent, and far below the *caçadores* and the 95th were spread on the mountain side as skirmishers. They employed only two columns of attack. The one came straight against the Light Division, etc., etc."

(The other column was Marchand's which attacked Pack's Portuguese.)

★★★★★★

It is not clear why they should be withdrawn—their fire was required until the reserve regiments commenced operations, and the horses would probably have been killed if required to move them. Anyway, Napier says "the artillery drew back"—which perhaps refers to the gunners.

By the time the column had reached a point some 25 or 30 yards from the crest, the Anglo-Portuguese skirmishers had re-formed on the reverse side of the ridge, and the French column is said to have paused for a few minutes to regain order and get breath. The real fact probably was that they had encountered the wall of rock above referred to. Those in front could not advance further, and it was necessary to halt the whole column. As soon as it was found that the obstacle was passable further to the left, the column, no doubt, wheeled to the left and resumed its advance on the guns.

The appointed signal was then given by Gen. Craufurd as he retired from his rock, calling forward the 43rd and 52nd Regiments.

The bugles sounded, and they appeared in line along the crest and commenced firing volleys into the French column. They had time to deliver three volleys before the column succeeded in closing, but Portuguese accounts call it file firing. The head of the column came into collision with the right company of the 52nd and the left company of the 43rd, and was broken "as against a wall" (Napier).

At the same time the wings of these two regiments, reinforced by the 95th Rifles and other light troops, who had returned mostly to the right of the 43rd, advanced and overlapped the column on both sides—but more so on the English right than on the left, where there was not much suitable ground. The column was enveloped in fire, and part of it being wedged in the road, on one side being a steep bank, and on the other a deep gully, the leading survivors being met by those still advancing, the greatest disorder ensued.

The 43rd and 52nd Regiments, the 95th, and the 3rd Caçadores then charged the column with the bayonet, completing its defeat and driving it helter-skelter down the hill, some of the enemy falling into the gully, and the bulk making for the village.

The main body of the Allies did not pursue, but some companies did so, as did most of the light troops, who had orders to that effect. The guns also played on the leading fugitives as they struggled

111

This is close to the Windmill. The miller is standing in the exact position taken up by the late King of
Portugal in the manœuvres held some years ago on the
battlefield, when the battle was fought over again by the
Portuguese troops. His back is turned to the village of
Sula at the moment, and he is standing nearly where the
head of Simon's column arrived at the crest.

This is an interesting picture. The village in the central distance is Moira, the head-quarters of Masséna during the battle. On the left is the historic village of Sula. On the right is what may be Craufurd's Rock. From this point he probably observed the progress of the French attack. The French passed it before they were driven back. It is fifty paces to the (English) left front of the Windmill. There are two other rocks, not so large, on the right front of the Windmill, at twenty paces distance, behind which were probably three of Ross's guns; one of them is visible to the (E.) right of the miller in the preceding picture.

through Sula. The flight continued after passing the village, and some of the pursuers went on firing and bayoneting as far as the brook at the bottom of the ravine, where, however, they were stopped by the fire of the French artillery posted on the height beyond.

From the time that Craufurd signalled to the concealed regiments until the French reached the brook, it was estimated by George Napier of the 52nd Light Infantry that only twenty minutes elapsed, but I think it must have been less. Never was a repulse more decisive, and no further attack was attempted here. Gen. Simon and many others were taken prisoners, and the loss of the French was very great.

The Light Division had been much enraged at the untruthful and boastful despatches sent by Masséna to Napoleon regarding the fight on the Coa, but they now felt that their revenge was ample.

During the charge the King's German Legion was brought forward to the ground lately occupied by the Light Division, who fell in again on the sloping plain behind.

The Hanoverians threw off their knapsacks in expectation of a renewed attack, but it did not come, and there was only some desultory skirmishing; some of their companies passing through the Light Division and covering their retreat.

Marchand, taking advantage of a fog which came on at 8 a.m., continued, however, his efforts to gain ground on the English right of the "funnel ravine," but the road there would only accommodate three files abreast, the ground was steep and the troops spread themselves out in a pine wood on the left of the road.

When the fog lifted, they were discovered, and came under the fire of Pack's skirmishers, and of several batteries, certainly Ross's and Cleeve's and Passos', and probably of some of the guns on or near the high plateau, including a 3-pounder battery and Lawson's 9-pounder battery.

Ney was for some time in the front here, and at length ordered Marchand to retire.

There were some curious incidents in connection with Gen. Simon, who was wounded and taken prisoner along with his *aide-de-camp* in the attack on the Light Division. In spite of three wounds Gen. Simon was excited and furious, and after his capture insisted on being allowed to meet Gen. Craufurd in single combat.

It was, however, pointed out to him that he was already a prisoner, and that an acceptance of his proposals would therefore not show much wit. Wellington treated him with great courtesy. He was taken

In the centre the village of Sula, on the right Moira, Masséna's usual
position in the battle. In the foreground is the old road to the Porta da
Sulla. Simon's route up the hill is to the left.

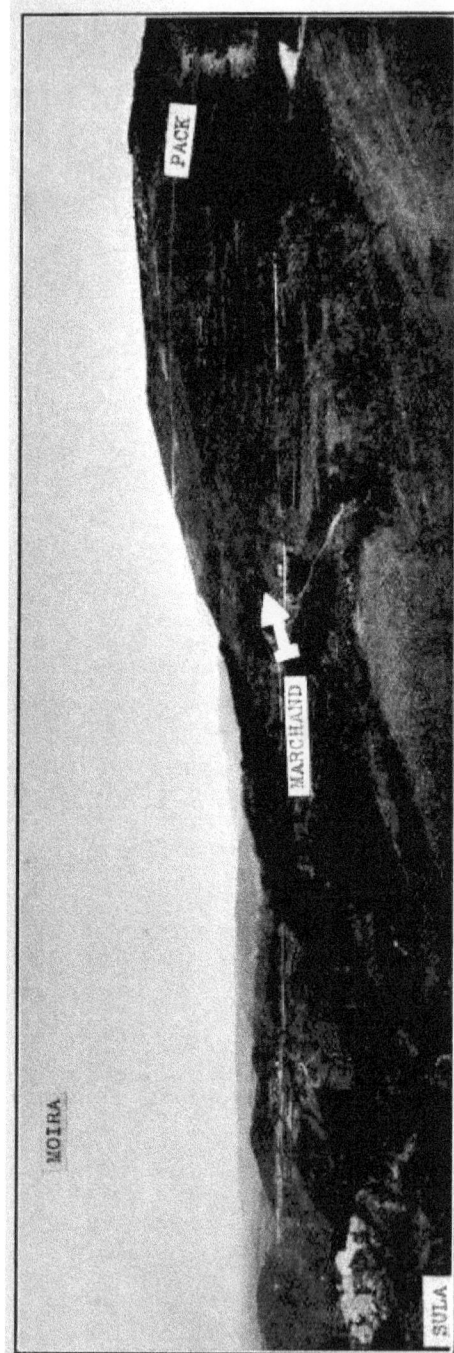

To show the difficulty of the ground attempted to be carried by Marchand, and defended by Pack's Portuguese.

to the convent, an English officer gave up his room, and the general's wounds were attended to. Word was also sent to Masséna, asking for his baggage to be sent.

In the meantime, his valet was endeavouring to penetrate the Allied lines, but his object being misunderstood, he was fired on. Thereupon, a French account says, the *cantinière* of the 26th Regiment of the line in Simon's Brigade, a young and pretty woman, hearing the complaint of the valet, insisted on loading her donkey with the general's kit, and proceeded towards the front, saying, "Let us see whether the English will kill a woman." She was allowed to pass without molestation, and was taken to the convent, where she remained until Gen. Simon and his *aide-de-camp* left for Coimbra next day, when she returned to her regiment.

An English officer, writing from the front under date 30th September, 1810, says that a short time after Simon was captured a young Spanish lady in male attire, whom the general had carried off from Madrid, and his baggage, were sent to the British headquarters under a flag of truce. The friar in his *Diary* says the French general, his wife, and secretary left for Coimbra on the 28th. Col. Leach says:

> Towards evening a flag of truce came in, bringing General Simon's baggage, and with it a pretty little Spanish woman, part of his establishment. The fair one was in tears, and appeared much agitated.

I cannot help thinking one of the above incidents gave rise to the story told by Napier of a Portuguese girl, young and handsome, who, he says, was seen coming from the French lines driving her donkey, "no man being so brutal as to interfere with her."

Simon's three wounds on the face were inflicted by shrapnel, but the bullets were so easily extracted and hurt him so little that Wellington's high opinion of the value of shrapnel at this time was shaken— *vide Supplementary Despatches*, Vol. VII:

> I have spoken to Sir W. Beresford and shall speak to General Graham, respecting Shrapnel's shells. I have seen our artillery produce great effect on the enemy, and I have been induced to attribute this effect to the use of Shrapnel's shells. But my opinion in favour of these shells has been much shaken lately.
>
> 1st. I have reason to believe that their effect is confined to wounds of a very trifling description, and they kill nobody.

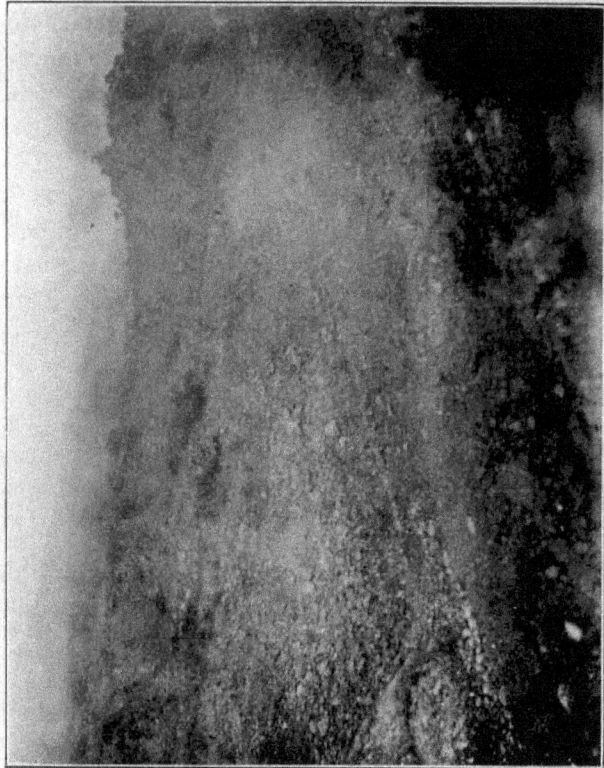

From here to Allied left is a ledge of rock.

Craufurd's rock.

Road

Road

Craufurd's position. Time exposure in a fog in the early morning. In front can be seen the French road up the hill. Craufurd's big rock is in the centre at the top of the picture.

I saw General Simon, who was wounded by the balls from Shrapnel's shells, of which he had several in the face and head; but they were picked out of his face as duck shot would be out of the face of a person who had been hit by accident while out shooting, and he was not much more materially hurt.

2nd. From the difficulty of judging of direct distances, and in knowing the shell has burst in the air in the proper place, I suspect that an original error in throwing the shells is seldom corrected; and that if the shell is not effective the first shot the continuance of the fire of these shells seldom becomes more effectual. I can entertain no doubt, however, that if the shell should be accurately thrown, and burst as it is intended, it must wound a great number of men, but probably none very materially.

Simon recovered and was sent to England from Lisbon in the *Apollo* frigate, which took only four days to reach Portsmouth, where it arrived on the 19th October, 1810. He gave his parole and was sent to live at Odiham in Hampshire, but he disgracefully broke it, and entered into a scheme with a French doctor and the French Government, for the purpose of liberating all the French prisoners in England. The general and the doctor were apprehended in a back kitchen of a Frenchwoman in Pratt Street, Camden Town, on the 15th January, 1812, with a number of fugitive prisoners. These were sent to the hulks, and Simon was made a close prisoner at Dumbarton on the Clyde. (See note on *French Prisoners in England*, in Appendix.)

Gen. Sir George T. Napier, in his work *Passages in my Early Military Life*, gives a spirited account of the part he took in the above repulse of the French, and it is given below *in extenso*:

We were retired a few yards from the brow of the hill, so that our line was concealed from the view of the enemy as they advanced up the heights, and our skirmishers retired, keeping up a constant and well-directed running fire upon them; and the brigade of Horse Artillery, under Capt. Hugh Ross, threw such a heavy fire of shrapnel shells, and so quick, that their column, which consisted of about 8,000 men, was put into a good deal of confusion and lost great numbers before it arrived at a ledge of ground just under the brow of the hill, where they halted a few minutes to take breath, the head of the column being exactly fronting my company, which was the right company of our brigade, and joining the left company of the 43rd, where my brother William was with his company.

General Craufurd himself stood on the brow of the hill watching every movement of the attacking column, and when all our skirmishers had passed by and joined their respective corps, and the head of the enemy's column was within a very few yards of him he turned round, came up to the 52nd and called out, *'Now, 52nd, revenge the death of Sir John Moore! Charge, Charge, Huzza!'* and, waving his hat in the air, he was answered by a shout which appalled the enemy, and in one instant the brow of the hill bristled with 2,000 British bayonets wielded by steady English hands, which soon buried them in the bodies of the fiery Gaul. (For a story relating to Capt. W. Jones of the 52nd Regiment, *vide* Appendix.)

My company met the head of the French column, and immediately calling to my men to form column of sections in order to give more force to our rush, we darted forward; and as I was by this movement in front of my men a yard or two, a French soldier made a plunge at me with his bayonet, and at the same time his musket going off I received the contents just under my hip and fell. At the same instant the French fired upon my front section, consisting of about nine men in the front rank, *all of whom fell*, four of them dead, the rest wounded; so that most probably by my being a little advanced in front my life was saved, as the men killed were exactly those nearest to me. Poor Colonel Barclay also received a severe wound, of which he afterwards died in England.

I got upon my legs immediately again and pursued the enemy down the hill, for by this time they had been completely repulsed, and were running away as fast as their legs would carry them. William and his friend Captain Lloyd, who were upon my right, seeing that the French were still in column and in great confusion from the unexpected suddenness of the charge and the shot which accompanied it, had wheeled up their companies by the left, and thus flanked the French column, and poured a well-directed fire right into them.

Major Arbuthnott, who was on my left, did the same with the remaining companies of the 52nd, so that the enemy was beset on both flanks of his column, and as you may suppose the slaughter was great. We kept firing and bayoneting until we reached the bottom, and the enemy passed the brook and fell back upon their main body—which moved down to support them and cover their retreat. All this was done in a very short time, that is, it was not above twenty minutes from the charge till the French were driven from the top to the bottom of the mountain like a parcel of sheep.

I really did not think it was possible for such a column to be so completely destroyed in a few minutes as that was, particularly after witnessing how gallantly they moved up under a destructive fire from the Artillery and a constant galling one from our Sharpshooters.

We took some prisoners, and among them General Simon, a gallant officer, but a bad and dishonourable man, who afterwards broke his parole of honour.

He was horribly wounded in the face, his jaw being broken and almost hanging down on his chest. Just as myself and another officer came to him a soldier was going to put his bayonet into him, which we prevented and sent him a prisoner to the general. As I went down the hill following the enemy, I saw seven or eight French officers lying wounded. One of them as I passed caught hold of my little silver canteen and implored me to stop and give him a drink, but much as it pained me to refuse, I could not do it, being in full pursuit of the enemy and it was impossible to stop for an instant. This may be thought hard-hearted, but in war we often do and *must* do many harsh and unfeeling things.

Had I stopped to give him a drink I must have done so for the others, and then I should have been the last at the bottom of the hill instead of one of the first in pursuit of the enemy; and recollect, my boys, that an officer should always be *first* in advancing against the enemy, and *last* in retreating from them.

When we got to the bottom, where a small stream ran between us and the enemy's position, by general consent we all mingled together searching for the wounded.

During this cessation of fighting we spoke to each other as though we were the greatest friends, and without the least animosity or angry feeling. One poor German officer in the French Army came to make enquiries about his brother who was in our service in the 60th Regiment, which was at that time composed principally of foreigners, and upon looking about he *found him dead*, the *poor fellow having been killed*.

121

Very soon Lord Wellington, finding we remained, as he thought, too long below, ordered the bugles to sound the retreat, and the French General having done the same, off scampered the soldiers of each army and returned to their several positions like a parcel of schoolboys called in from play by their masters. I was so stiff by this time that I had difficulty in walking up the hill again, and was obliged to get Mr. Winterbottom, the adjutant of the regiment, to help me up.

When I arrived at the top, I understood that my brother Charles was severely wounded in the face while attending Lord Wellington during the battle, and that he was gone, or rather carried, to the rear, attended by our cousin, Captain Charles Napier, of the navy, who had been with us for some weeks as an assistant, not having a ship at that time, and being too active and interfering a fellow to remain at home idle waiting for me. He had gone out with me to the enemy before the battle to skirmish a little with the French pickets, as General Craufurd thought they had advanced rather closer to the front of our position than was right, so I was ordered to move down and put them a little further off.

Charles Napier, our cousin, *would* take a little white pony I had, to ride with us, notwithstanding I told him it was very foolish, for most certainly he would get hit, being the only person on horseback. But he chose to go his own way, and in less than half an hour he got shot in the calf of the leg, but very slightly, and I was delighted at it—the obstinate dog—he deserved it well. However, he was very good-humoured, and laughed as much as anyone at his own folly. William had escaped being wounded in the battle—and he and I were very glad to find ourselves side by side again.

In about half an hour after we returned to our position the whole army was under arms and Lord Wellington rode along the line receiving a cheer from every regiment as he passed. While in the act of doing this, I am sorry to say, the French general did a most unhandsome thing, and that was to make one of his batteries to fire at Lord Wellington as he rode along accompanied by his staff. This was shameful and cowardly, because Marshal Masséna knew (the thing was too evident for him not to know) that he was only reviewing and thanking his troops for their bravery, and he should have prevented any such act.

The village of Sula from a little in front of the Porta da Sulla. Craufurd's position on the left is not visible.

Had Marshal Soult or Marshal Ney been the General in Command of the French Army, they would have scorned such an act.

It will be seen that the accounts given above are quite different from the story as told by Prof. Oman, in his recent work on the Peninsular War. I have, however, come to the conclusion that the latter writer is mistaken in the following points:—

First, about the main road.—He appears to think that the present *chaussée* existed at the date of the battle. The roads as existing are shown on my plans—the main road did not sweep round the head of the funnel ravine and pass on to the height by a cleft. This is, in my opinion, a modern work. There was therefore no cutting in which the 43rd and 52nd and 1st Caçadores could lie down; moreover, the present cutting is about fifteen feet deep, mostly in rock or hard material, and is only climbable in places. There was no necessity, moreover, for the troops to hide themselves in the cutting. Sir George Napier correctly states that they were only "*a few yards from the brow, so that our line was concealed from the view of the enemy as they advanced up the heights*" The accompanying photograph of the reverse side of Craufurd's position shows this clearly to be correct (*vide* details picture chapter 4).

Secondly.—Prof. Oman gives two maps of the French right attack—in the larger one the village of Sula is marked on the modern *chaussée*, while on the smaller map it is marked 500 metres away from it.

Thirdly.—Prof. Oman, in the latter map, shows the Allies lying on the *chaussée* having a front of 365 metres, while he allots the French a frontage of 600 metres. In his description he quite correctly says the Allies overlapped the French column. How would this be possible if the allied front was so much less than that of the French?

Fourthly.—The Professor shows the French, under Simon and Ferey, advancing in 6 columns. The accounts of the battle handed down to us are practically unanimous in describing the French as attacking in one solid column. William Napier and others admit, however, that there might have been a flanking detachment on the French left, but I have been unable to discover any authority for Prof. Oman's 6 columns.

The great French column was, after passing Sula apparently, in column of companies, *i.e.* each company had 3 ranks of about 30 men each, taking a company as consisting of 90 men—if in each battalion there were 567 officers and men there would be an average of 6 companies of 90 men each—or 18 ranks in a battalion. Each company would require, including distances between companies, a space of about 8 yards from front to rear, so that a battalion would require 40 yards + 10 yards to the next battalion—50 yards x 10 battalions, 40 yards x 1 battalion, *i.e.*—

$$
\begin{array}{ll}
10 \times 50= & 500 \\
1 \times 40= & 40 \\
\hline
& 540 \text{ yards} \\
\hline
\end{array}
$$

=540 yards for the division—assuming that one battalion had formed a left flanking detachment.

Now the distance from the entrance of the village of Sula to the position of Ross's guns by the French route was about 450 yards, so that the rear of the column (when the head reached the guns' position and all ranks had closed up to the proper distances) would not be clear of the village.

There is another doubtful point in Prof. Oman's account—I refer to his statement in Vol. III, —

Simon's front regiment, the 26th of the line, stuck to the mule path up the hill from Sula in one dense and deep column with the front of a company only and a depth of 3 battalions.

His plan, however, shows them as having 1 battalion on the right, 3 in the centre, and 2 on their left—*i.e.* 3 columns, so that the text seems to contradict the plan.

Then, later, it is stated that when the French had captured Sula, they:

....found themselves under a heavy fire of artillery; Ross's guns on the knoll above, between their embrasures of rock, being carefully trained upon the exits of the village, *while Cleeve's German battery joined in from its position at the head of the ravine* and took Ferey in flank. It was impossible to halt in Sula.

I can find no warrant for the statement in italics. They might have attacked the flanking detachment defeated by the 19th Portuguese. These guns could see Sula, but not the ascending road, and in order to attack the French flank as alleged, it would have been necessary to fire haphazard over the shoulder, which would have been destructive to

This is taken from below Pack's position, and shows the sort of wood occupied by Marchand. In the background is Sula; on the left the slope up which Loison's troops attacked Craufurd.

the Allied light troops, who had to retire up the slope and were very near to the French all the time.

On the other hand, there is evidence that Bull's guns on Craufurd's left helped Ross's battery in the attack.

Bull was nearer than Cleeve—had a direct view of what was going on, and could and did support Ross effectively—Cleeve was over 800 yards off from the French, a hill intervened which, along with the fog and smoke, would make the value of Cleeve's support problematical; besides which he had Marchand to attend to—and Major McBean was informed by the artillery officers that they were firing on the main body of the enemy, which must surely have been the strong column advancing under Marchand's command at that time along the main road.

It may be here remarked that Prof. Oman's mistake about the main road leads to another error as to Ross's battery. It appears to me that on his plan it is given an incorrect position to the extent of about 200 yards. It was really on the brow of the hill, behind the rocks over-looking Sula—and not as this plan shows it, in front of the modern *chaussée*, where the guns would be useless when most wanted. The position of the Light Division, as shown by Prof. Oman, is also affected by the mistake about the road, to the extent of about 250 yards.

Referring again to the question of the resistance offered at Sula to the French advance, General Fane says that:

> Sula was ceded with little opposition—this village, though of importance to the allied army, was *without* the position in which Lord Wellington had determined to receive the enemy's attack; he therefore abandoned it, choosing rather to suffer some annoyance from its possession by the enemy than risk the chance of an action to maintain it, in less advantageous ground than the position he had fixed on.

However, the French were not wanted there *after* the battle; and were turned out of it by Craufurd.

Napier states that at two o'clock both armies ceased fighting and mixed together, carrying off wounded men; and that towards evening a French company, with signal audacity, seized a village only half-musket shot from the Light Division and refused to retire, whereupon Craufurd turned twelve guns on the intruders and overwhelmed them with bullets for half an hour; but after paying the French captain this distinguished honour recovered his temper, and sent a company of the 43rd down, which cleared the village in a few minutes. Col. Leach says it was a company of the 95th Rifles, that did this. This must have been the village of Sula, or Sulla.

It was the idea of Masséna to draw the Allies into a fight on ground more favourable than that chosen by Wellington, but this and other such attempts failed in their object, as Wellington's commanders steadily kept in view the inadvisability of reinforcing their skirmishing line too freely, and when pressed the light troops almost invariably retired—that evening and on the following day. Of course, Sula was in itself untenable by the French, but a commander might have come to grief had he incautiously been drawn by the French into an engagement below that village.

The losses suffered by Simon's Brigade were as follows:

26th Ligne	1,625	283 = 17·4%
Légion du Midi	564	311 = 55%
Légion Hanovrienne	1,158	217 = 13.74%

In referring to the sudden attack by the Light Division, Koch, in his *Life of Masséna*, page 197, states that the Légion du Midi, the 26th Ligne, and the Légion Hanovrienne resisted the shock.

As he mentions the Legion du Midi first, and as they suffered such a terrific loss, it looks as though this was the leading battalion, but Prof. Oman says that the 26th Ligne were leading, for which there is certainly one authority, that of Colonel Delagrave.

Baron Fririon, Chief of Staff to Masséna, in *Journal Historique de la Campagne de Portugal*, states that General Simon was wounded and made prisoner when about to capture the battery, *at the head of his tirailleurs.*

Colonel Delagrave, in his *Memoirs:*

Simon, at the head of the 26th Line, had captured three pieces of cannon. '*Appelées pour garnir le terrain les légions du Midi et Hanovrienne se débandèrent.*'

However, the English practice was to attack the head of a French column principally—and I think the Légion du Midi must have been the leading battalion—whilst the 26th Ligne might have furnished the *tirailleurs*, at the head of which Simon tried to capture the battery.

Note.—With reference to Junot's statement, referred to elsewhere, Anthony Hamilton, of the 43rd Regiment, stated in his book, *Campaigns with Moore and Wellington*, as follows:

The attack of Ney was even less successful. With a division of his corps in column of mass he advanced against the height occupied by our (the Light) division. General Pack's brigade of Portuguese was also placed here, and we were ordered to change coats with them in order to deceive the enemy.

I am not aware of any confirmation, except the above, of Junot's statement, that such an exchange of clothes was made by the Allies. As the 43rd were lying down behind the crest the French could not see them, and would not be deceived with respect to that regiment. Pack's Portuguese were not nearer to the Light Division than half a mile, and the marching of one of their regiments to Craufurd's position, for such a purpose, would have attracted a good deal of notice, and would surely have been referred to by Napier, or some other officer of the division, in one of the numerous books or diaries which have been published. Though possibly, if it was done, it might not have been thought well to publish the fact.

After describing the charge of the 43rd and 52nd Regiments, Anthony Hamilton (43rd) says that:

While endeavouring to regain the hill, I ran into a house (village of Sula) that was deserted, in order to avoid their fire (that of the French guns) for a moment, and while there I observed the end of a sword hanging from the chimney just below the jamb. Thinking there must be an owner to it, I looked up the chimney, and discovered a French officer, who had hid there to escape pursuit. I immediately pulled him down and told him that he was my prisoner, upon which he took out a gold watch and gave it to me if I would release him. I immediately took the watch, and was leaving in a hurry, when, unfortunately for the Frenchman, I met another soldier at the door, who, however, consented to let him go upon his giving him his gold epaulets. A very curious incident occurred before we charged the enemy upon the ascent. While they were advancing up the hill a field officer was observed upon a very fine horse at a short distance from the main body. A private of our regiment (the 43rd), by the name of Carroll, asked permission of his captain to go and take possession of the officer's horse. The captain readily gave his permission, though laughing at the idea, and the soldier sprang out of the ranks towards the enemy, waving his shako upon his bayonet. The enemy, surprised and thinking perhaps that he was the bearer of some message, or something of the kind, did not fire upon him, and running up to the officer as about to communicate something, he seized him by the leg, and being a very strong man, threw him instantly upon the ground. Throwing himself quickly upon the horse, he rode back into our ranks amid the cheers of his comrades.

Note Regarding the Formation of Loison's Division in the Attack on Craufurd's Division.

The accounts of British writers usually describe Loison's division as a column, a single column, or a great column. The French accounts say it was assembled "*en masse par brigades.*" Soldiers whom I have consulted look upon this as meaning that each regiment, of which there were six, was formed in columns of companies, and that one regiment was behind the other—that is, formed in a column of regiments—but it is possible that after passing Sula village three regiments were abreast, *i.e.* having a front of ninety men, and that the other three regiments were in rear of them in a similar formation, but the road would not have accommodated them.

This *might* be described by the British officers as a column—but I do not think we can say with any confidence that the British officers would have described the division as being a column of any kind, *if the French had advanced with each regiment in column of companies and the six regiments in line,* that is with a total front of 180 men with intervals between regiments.

Whether such columns were in line, or in echelon, I think they would have been described as six columns—and not as a column, a single column, or a great column.

A column implies length from front to rear, and such a formation as is last described would give an idea of breadth, rather than of depth. Moreover, General Sir George T. Napier says that when "the head of the enemy's column was within a very few yards of him (Craufurd) he turned round, came up to the 52nd and called out, 'Now, 52nd, revenge the death of Sir John Moore.'" Napier goes on to say, "My company met the head of the French column, and, immediately calling to my men to form column of sections in order to give more force to our rush, we darted forward."

Sir William Napier says:

Ney employed two columns of attack (*i.e.* Marchand's and Loison's). The one came straight against the Light Division; the head of it, striking the right company of the 52nd and the left company of the 43rd, was broken as against a wall.

These two quotations seem convincing as to the breadth of the French attack not being great. If Sir George Napier's one company in sections could attack the head of the French column it must have had a comparatively narrow head; certainly, such an attack would have been useless against a many-headed column.

It is necessary to refer here to the statement of Lt.-Colonel J. Leach, C.B., at that time in the 95th Regiment.

He says that a considerable portion of Ney's infantry advanced by the road leading to the crest where the Light Division was in line. After describing its repulse, he says:

It can be readily conceived, that so large a column, wedged in a road of no great width, being once broken and forced back, those pressing on from the rear to support it, were literally borne back down the mountain by the tide of fugitives, in spite of any exertions of theirs to retrieve matters."

Up to this we hear of only "*a column*" it will be observed; but the next sentence is, "*The instant the attacking columns were turned back they were exposed to the fire of our whole division*"; and in the next paragraph he says, "*The village of Sula, and the ground on each side of it, as also the road by which the columns of attack advanced, were heaped with killed and wounded.*"

It must, I think, be inferred from above that *the column* was composed of a number of parts, all of which advanced by the road—so that there must have been intervals between the parts composing the great column, which agrees with the view that the French advanced up or near the road in column of companies by regiments one behind the other; or, as it is described, in mass by brigades; but I see no reason why they should not have been in column of route, perhaps in sections, with the usual intervals. Certainly, they could not pass through the narrow street of Sula in columns of companies, nor could they even march from Moira to Sula in that formation.

CHAPTER 11

The Attack by the 19th Portuguese Line Regiment on One of Ney's Columns, or on a Strong Body of the Enemy's Sharpshooters

When Gen. Simon and Ferey, under Gen. Loison's command, commenced their attack, by Sula, on the Light Division, it was arranged that Gen. Marchand should support them by an advance along the main road which ran towards the heights on the south side of the funnel ravine.

These attacks were apparently connected by some part of the troops of Gen. Ferey's division. It is not clear what portion. The division consisted of the

	Officers.	Men.	
32nd Leger, 2nd Battalion	20	393=	413
66th Ligne, 4th, 5th, and 6th Battalions	68	1,762 =	1,830
82nd Ligne, 4th and 6th Battalions	40	1,196 =	1,236
			3479

We do not know for certain what portion attacked the Light Division, along with Simon, nor what portion formed a flanking detachment. Col. Delagrave, in his *Memoirs*, states that the whole of this division engaged the brigade of Coleman, but no other writer confirms it.

It seems likely that part of the division did engage Coleman, but

This shows the new Chaussée which goes round the "funnel ravine" and enters Craufurd's position in deep cutting just to the left of the Windmill. I do not think the wood near the cutting existed at the time of the battle. The 3-pounder battery, Cleeve's 6-pounders, and Parros's 6-pounders were all to the left of this position round the head of the ravine. It will be seen that the hill intervened between them and Loison's attack. The village of Sula is just visible on the right. This picture is taken from ground much lower than Craufurd's position, near the extreme front reached by Marchand's skirmishers.

only a part. The bulk was involved in Simon's repulse by Craufurd.

Part of Ferey's division appears to have advanced up the ravine on its right side from near Sula.

Such an advance would come under the fire of Cleeve's K.G.A. Battery and other guns placed at the head of the ravine near Craufurd's right flank, and that of Pack's Portuguese skirmishers.

Coleman's Independent Portuguese Brigade was at this time drawn up in front of the convent eastern wall, between the Porta da Sulla and Craufurd, and were near the Portuguese 3-pounder battery.

Before them was a short plain gradually inclining to the edge of the steep descent of the hill.

One of Ney's columns having succeeded in ascending the steep formed and advanced upon the plain. When about halfway up the 19th Portuguese Regiment charged them with the bayonet, and drove them headlong down the steep: a heavy (French) battery opened upon them (the 19th Portuguese) from the opposite side of the ravine; the regiment immediately, under the fire, reformed, faced to the right about, and as if manoeuvring on a parade, regained its original position, amid the acclamations of all the left of the British Army who were spectators of their conduct. (Beresford).

Major-Gen. Sir William MacBean, at that time a Lieut.-Colonel commanding the 19th Portuguese Regiment, referring to the above, says:

The enemy had just commenced to advance, but seeing us pass through the pickets returned to his position (*i.e.* on the road), where he attempted to maintain himself, but the 19th continued to move on, gave him a volley and charged, when the lines became mixed; the result was soon decided, the enemy being driven with considerable loss in killed and wounded to the bottom of the ravine.

MacBean says he then brought the battalion back to its other wing, which had remained in front of the wall, under Gen. Coleman, who gave MacBean a most flattering reception; and the troops round cheered as the battalion returned.

The 19th Portuguese lost—8 men killed, 28 men and 1 officer wounded; total, 37.

The whole regiment numbered 1,124, so if we take each battalion

Monumento.   CRAUFURD.   Road.   Road.

The "funnel ravine," showing old road from Moira to Sula village—probable site of Macbean's charge with 19th Portuguese.

as numbering 562, the above loss works out to 6½ *per cent* for the battalion of 5 companies engaged.

Now we know the total losses of Ferey's Brigade on this day to have been as follows:

Strength.	Batt.		Killed Off.	Killed Men.	Wounded Off.	Wounded Men.
413	1	32nd Leger	2	13	3	95 = 113 or 27·4 %
1,830	3	66th Ligne	5	15	15	123 = 158 or 8·6 %
1,236	2	82nd Ligne	3	18	4	145 = 170 or 13·8 %
						441

The average is 127 *per cent* on 3,479 officers and men. The 32nd Leger seems to have had a different experience from the others. Col. Delagrave's statement identifies the troops engaging Coleman, and the above looks as if the 32nd Leger did so engage the 19th Portuguese. If the 32nd had been part of the huge column which attacked Craufurd they would have been more than half-way to Sula when the column was defeated, and we know of nothing which would tend to make their loss (if there) double that of any of the other regiments in the division (except the Légion du Midi).

Their loss of 27.4 *per cent* was a heavy one, and if this corps was actually concerned in the attack on the Light Division, some of the 113 men they had killed and wounded would almost certainly have been noticed by Lieut.-Col. J. Leach, at that time an officer in the 95th Regiment. He says he made an examination of those who had fallen immediately in front of his division, and he found men of the following French regiments:

6th, 26th, 66th, 82nd, Legion du Midi and Légion Hanovrienne. The last he calls "a German regiment."

It will be noticed that he mentions every regiment of Simon's and Ferey's Brigades, except the 32nd Leger.

Though this evidence is not quite conclusive, it is much in favour of the idea that the 32nd Leger was the regiment which the 19th Portuguese defeated further to the French left.

Sir B. D'Urban confirms portions of MacBean's narrative, and says the charge was a matter of notoriety at the time, and that he had never before (1833) heard it questioned.

Southey, in his history, says:

Some of the Portuguese charging a *superior* force got so wedged in among the French that they had not room to use their bayo-

The cartroad from Sula towards the Porta da Sulla, possibly taken by 32nd Leger, though it is possible that they took the main road back towards Moira, which at first runs in nearly the same direction.

nets. They turned up the butt ends of their muskets and plied them with such vigour, that they promptly cleared the way. Never was a battle fought of more eventual importance to the Portuguese nation.

Lord Wellington, in his despatch of the 30th September, 1810, to the Portuguese Secretary for War, says:

On the left side the enemy attacked with 3 divisions of infantry of the 8th Corps (should be 6th) that part of the Serra occupied by the Light Division, commanded by Brigadier-General Craufurd, and by a Portuguese Brigade commanded by General Pack.

One single division of the enemy's infantry made some progress in the ascent towards the top of the Serra when they were immediately charged with the bayonet by Brig.-General Craufurd, with the 43rd, 52nd, and 95th Regiments and the regiment of Portuguese Caçadores No. 3, and obliged to retreat with immense loss.

A brigade of Portuguese Infantry under the command of General Coleman, which was in reserve, was moved to support on the right the division of General Craufurd; and one battalion of the Portuguese 19th Regiment, commanded by Lt.-Colonel MacBean, made a resolute and very successful attack against a corps of another division of the enemy that had tried to penetrate in that same place.

Marshal Beresford in his despatch of the 30th September, 1810, to the Secretary for War, Portuguese Government, says:

A brigade of Brig.-Genl. Coleman, the 7th and 19th and the 2nd Caçadores merit praise for their conduct, and particularly 5 companies of the 19th Regt., under the immediate orders of Lt.-Col. MacBean, made an attack with the bayonet upon the enemy, and what is particularly made mention of by all the officers of both armies that they returned back in a perfect manner, (admirable) as much by their discipline as by the valour they showed.

"Order of the Day" by Adjt.-Gen. Manuel de Pinto Mousinho, 28th September, 1810, at Bussaco.

A good charge made by 5 companies of the 19th Regiment

under the immediate orders of Lt.-Col. MacBean merits to be particularised, and was admired by all the army.

Sir John Burgoyne, who was present at Bussaco, says:

> In the course of the day the 1st (*sic*) Portuguese Regiment of the Line distinguished itself by advancing down the hill in line, and driving a strong body of the enemy from the road, and the 4th Regt. of Caçadores behaved also with great spirit, and was handled with great skill. In short, in all parts where they had an opportunity, the Portuguese Regiments of the Line and the Artillery behaved very well.

We will now summarise the descriptions of the enemy that was defeated by the 19th Portuguese.

> Fririon says the division Loison disposed in mass by brigades attacked the enemy by *two* paths which "*bordaient la route.*"
> Delagrave states that Gen. Ferey with the 32nd Leger, 66th and 82nd Line, engaged the brigade of Coleman (to which the 19th Portuguese belonged).
>
> Beresford.—"One of Ney's columns."
>
> MacBean.—"The enemy."
>
> Wellington.—"A corps of another division of the enemy" (*i.e.* not of Loison's Division).
>
> Burgoyne.—"Driving a strong body of the enemy from the road."
>
> Napier—"The skirmishers, or a small flanking detachment from the column which attacked the Light Division, might have passed under the edge of the descent on the right of the Light Division, and gathering in a like manner have risen under General MacBean's line."
>
> Sturgeon.—"About nine o'clock the enemy pushed forward his sharpshooters, in very considerable numbers, to a rocky eminence in front of the right regiment of Coleman's brigade, but that regiment repulsed them, and the whole of the brigade made a forward movement till recalled by Lord Wellington."

In face of the conflict of evidence we cannot be sure that the 32nd Leger was repulsed by the 19th Portuguese; but the latter evidently deserved all the credit it got from Lord Wellington.

It may be here remarked that the strongest evidence against the theory that the enemy's troops consisted of the 32nd Leger is the time mentioned by Major Sturgeon for the occurrence, *viz*. 9 a.m.; at the same time it is not conclusive evidence, as the 32nd Leger would almost certainly (if once committed to the "funnel ravine") have got mixed up with the *tirailleurs* of other regiments, and would have made slow progress in this complicated ground.

The "rocky eminence" is still a conspicuous object.

NOTE AS TO THE BATTLE POSITION OF COLEMAN'S PORTUGUESE BRIGADE.

Prof. Oman, Vol. 1, states as follows:

North of them (the Guards) again, where the ridge falls sharply along the back wall of the convent wood, was Pack's Portuguese brigade, reaching almost to the high road. Along the curve of the high road itself, in column, was Coleman's Portuguese brigade, etc.

In reading this we must bear in mind that the writer of it is under a misapprehension as to the position of the old high road running past the convent wall from Moira. The present Chaussee is not the same road as existed at the date of the battle. Pack's position was too high for any proximity to the old high road, and Coleman's position was not on the existing road, but as Major Sturgeon expresses it, "In column, as a reserve, between the park wall and the Chapel of Almas de Incarnador." It was, in fact, not far from the Porta da Rainha, and not as Prof. Oman shows it, half-way down the new road to Lugo. This was their first position.

Major Sturgeon says:

Coleman's Portuguese Brigade had also moved forward in column, towards that part of the position, on the right of the Light Division, where the Portuguese 3-pounders were: and it afterwards formed in line, in front of the eastern park wall of the convent, where the abattis in front of the gate, as well as the wall on each side of it, was lined with musketry.

CHAPTER 12

The Artillery at Bussaco

Duncan in his *History of the Royal Artillery*, writes as follows:

In the battle which followed, Lord Wellington displayed an ignorance of artillery tactics, from the result of which he was happily saved by the intelligence and gallantry of the representatives of that arm. This want of knowledge, which he never overcame, was the cause of a not unfrequent irritation against artillery as an arm, and a tendency to depreciate its value.

This denunciation seems to me, on the facts, to be a little strong. After reading it, one would naturally expect to find following it some very excellent reasons for the charge, but the paragraph continues as follows:

At Bussaco, instead of massing his Artillery in reserve until the attack should develop itself, the guns were placed as a rule in the easiest parts of the position where it was supposed the French would attack; and they were massed in these positions so as to form an excellent mark for the enemy's fire. This was more especially the case with Major Arentschildt's 6-pr. and 9-pr. brigades of Portuguese Artillery. Fortunately, the artillery was well served, and as Sir John Burgoyne wrote, 'the guns had great effect.'

The writer of above, then, thinks that the whole of the guns available should have been massed in reserve somewhere, and only when the attack had developed should they have been brought into action.

I have no hesitation in saying that this was an absolute impossibility.

The position was about eleven miles long—and the above writer apparently thinks that the *probable* points of attack should have been ignored.

Assume first, then, the extreme case that the guns had been massed on the right, and that the attack was made on the left, it would have taken, on such roads as existed, many hours for the guns to get into action from the commencement of the attack, if they could get there even the same day, for the condition laid down above is that they were not to move until the attack had developed, and they would then have to travel over almost impassable places at one extremity.

Second, if the guns were massed on the left, and the attack was made on the right, a similar thing would happen.

Third, if the guns were massed in the centre, and if the attack were made on both flanks, the guns would be divided and sent to the points attacked. As, again, this would only have been properly done, according to the writer, when the attack had developed, the guns would have been in action opposite Cole's Division perhaps in an hour after the attack commenced, and if the attack had been at the Gondolem and Carvalhos road, across the Serra, which was expected, the guns would have taken about six hours or more to get into action.

Major Dickson says that he was never able to get more than two of his guns before the fighting was over to the S. Antonio do Cantaro Pass, from the extreme right of the Allied position.

It is clear, therefore, that an attack on the right or left flank could not be met in time by the Artillery if massed in the centre; and had the Artillery been massed in the centre, and been sent right and left to the S. Antonio do Cantaro Pass, and to Craufurd's position after the attacks there had been developed, it is extremely doubtful whether the guns would have arrived in time to be of any use, especially in the case of the attack on Craufurd, which was over so quickly.

On the morning of the 27th September, though it was at first clear, the view of the battlefield was at intervals afterwards obscured by fogs, and as the French were not likely to do much with their artillery, I think Wellington, or more likely his chief artillery officer, Brig.-Gen. Haworth, (sometimes spelt Howorth, which is possibly correct), did the right thing in distributing the artillery along the line at intervals, so as to ensure superiority over the enemy on this arm at every likely point of attack.

Duncan says that Wellington was saved from the effects of his ignorance by the intelligence and gallantry of the gunners, and by the fact that the guns were well served. Well, we expect these (and all other good qualities) in gunners, and we certainly expect them to serve their guns well. Perhaps Wellington did too, and, therefore knew what he was about.

Duncan quotes Sir John Burgoyne as to the "great effect of the guns," which shows they were well placed; but Sir John Burgoyne finds no fault with their positions. He says:

> From Bussaco (the convent) to the left there is a double ridge; the front one, and that most strongly occupied, is in an indented line, very favourable for obtaining a flanking fire of artillery. From Bussaco to the right at Pena Cova is in one sweep, affording few favourable points for defence by guns.

Capt. Lane, Second Captain of Thompson's Brigade, No. 6 of the 7th Battalion, R.A., says: "I will venture to assert that the greatest loss the enemy sustained was by our artillery"; and he quotes various remarks of officers present as to the great effect of the artillery.

If Wellington is supposed to have taken the responsibility of placing the artillery himself, in opposition to, or even without consulting, the senior artillery officer, surely he should, on either of these assumptions, have all or part of the credit of its alleged great success, but Wellington gives the credit in his despatch to Brig.-Gen. Haworth.

If the truth were known, we should probably find that the latter artillery officer was largely responsible for the location of the guns.

The number of guns used at Bussaco is a question of some difficulty.

Prof. Oman says sixty guns were distributed along the line:

R.H.A. Ross with Craufurd ..	..	6 guns
,, Bull with Cole	..	6 ,,
R.F.A. Lawson with Pack ..	..	6 ,,
,, Thompson with Lightburne		6 ,,
K.G.A. Rettberg's with Spencer	..	6 ,,
,, Cleeve's with Coleman	..	6 ,,
English and German	..	36 guns
1 Portuguese Field Battery at S. Antonio Pass under Major Arentschildt (His Appendix states 2 batteries of 3-prs.)		6 guns
Dickson's 2 batteries with Hill	..	12 ,,
Passos with Coleman alongside of Cleeve	..	6 ,,
		60 guns

Taking Prof. Oman's total of 60 guns, we must deduct 10 which Major Dickson says he could not get into action—50 guns; and add 4 which Leith says that he dropped at the Pass—total, 54 guns. But I make out that at least 66 guns were in action—and almost certainly 72.

It is a practical certainty that the Pass of S. Antonio do Cantaro would be strongly defended by artillery. Large numbers of French troops were known to be concentrated below it on the day before.

According to the map showing position of guns accompanying Vol. 13, *Proceedings of R.A. Institute*, only six guns were originally placed here; and Prof. Oman adopts this statement. It is stated, however, in Marshal Beresford's despatch to the Portuguese Secretary of War, dated Coimbra, 30th September, 1810, that "two brigades of artillery 9 and 6-pounders, under the personal orders of Major Arentschildt, much distinguished themselves," etc., whilst Sir John Burgoyne, an accurate writer, and Duncan, in his *History of the Royal Artillery*, both say that Major Arentschildt had two batteries there, one of 6-pounders, and one of 9-pounders, but they do not specify the hour they were seen there. Another writer (Grattan, Connaught Rangers) mentions that Major Von Arentschildt passed Lightburne's Brigade at daylight on the 27th, proceeding with a battery to the S. Antonio Pass.

Leith says he added one battery of four 6-pounders, and Dickson says he added two guns, which makes a total of eighteen guns, which perhaps accounts largely for the fact that all the attacks along this road were kept off by fire. On both sides of the road through the Pass were numberless boulders affording good cover to the troops, who were at the same time situated above the approaching enemy, and able to discern all their movements—so that with the strong support of the artillery it was not difficult to keep back the enemy.

We may take the artillery on the field of action to have been as follows:

With Gen. Hill, unable to get into action—Major Dickson 10 guns
_____

In action in the battle:

Portuguese	36 guns
British	24 ".
Hanoverian	12 "

_____

72 guns
_____

Which, with ten of Dickson's, not in action, and two of Leith's 6-pounders left at N. S. de Monte Alto, makes a total of eighty-four guns on the Serra. Prof. Oman says that one of Dickson's Portuguese batteries was with Leith.

Whether this was so, or not, Leith had his own Divisional Artillery which marched with him, and it is clear that he placed four of his 6-pounder guns at the S. Antonio do Cantaro Pass.

Prof. Oman, in his Appendix, says that the following Portuguese units were present at the Battle of Bussaco:

1st Regiment.—Two batteries under Major Alex. Dickson, *viz.* those of Capt. Pedro da Rozierres, Capt. Joao da Cunha Preto (both of 6-pounders).

2nd Regiment.—Two batteries under Major Von Arentschildt, *viz.* those of Capt. Joao Porfirio da Silva, Capt. Jacinto P. M. Freire (both of 3-pounders).
(Prof. Oman omits these guns altogether in his text describing the battle, and on his plans.)

4th Regiment.—One battery under Capt. Antonio de Songa Passos, of 6-pounders.

The above batteries, belonging to the 1st and 4th Regiments, we are able to locate on the field of battle, and two batteries of 3-pounders of the 2nd Regiment, under the command of Major Von Arentschildt are referred to hereafter.

I have seen no reference in Prof. Oman's work, or in any of the accounts written at any time by R.A. officers, to the location of these two batteries of 3-pounders.

If Major Von Arentschildt was in command of two batteries of 6-pounders and 9-pounders, as stated above and elsewhere, it would be interesting to learn which units they were. Prof. Oman's statement in his Appendix that this officer commanded two batteries of 3-pounders in the battle does not appear to be correct.

Major Sturgeon places them on or near the high plateau, *i.e.* near the centre.

Supplementary Despatches, XIII, gives Craufurd two R.H.A. batteries and one Portuguese 3-pounder battery; but all accounts agree that he had only one battery of R.H.A. (Ross's), and a 3-pounder battery is never mentioned as being with him in the battle.

The full list given in the *Despatches* is as follows:

	Guns.
1st Division (Spencer) 6 9-pr., 12 6-pr. British and German	18
Ditto, 6 6-pr. Portuguese	6
3rd Division (Picton), 6 9-pr., 6 6-pr. Portuguese	12
4th Division (Cole), 6 6-pr., British R.H.A.	6
Light Division (Craufurd), 12 6-pr., British R.H.A.	12
Ditto 6 9-pr. Portuguese.. ..	6
Gen. Hill (exclusive of 6 6-pr. with Col. le Cor—Portuguese)	12
Gen. Leith, 6 9-pr., 6 6-pr., Portuguese ..	12
	84

But Supplementary Despatches, in Wellington's *Memo, of Operations*, Vol. VII, February 23rd, 1881, states only six Portuguese batteries present, whereas there are eight given above.

My own impression is that Leith's 9-pounder battery was placed before the battle under Major Von Arentschildt, and afterwards was posted to Hill's Division, for it is mentioned in General Orders signed by Gen. Murray a few days after the battle that Gen. Leith's 9-pounder battery was now under Gen. Hill.

But Picton had Divisional Artillery, *vide* Despatches above quoted, and it is very likely that Major Von Arentschildt was deputed to command at the Pass owing to its great importance, while his 3-pounders, we know, were left behind in the centre.

The Q.M.G. in his Orders of 20th September, 1810, says:

The road being practicable for Portuguese Artillery, that which is attached to the 3rd Division will follow in rear of the Division.

The artillery officers and units at Bussaco whose identity can be traced are given on the next page.

If, however, as seems certain, Major Von Arentschild had a battery of Portuguese 6-pounders at the Pass before Leith's guns arrived, the total number must be increased to 72 guns in action, add 10 not arrived—82 guns: add 2 at Monte Alto. Total 84 guns.

It is necessary to make this note, as Sir John Burgoyne and Duncan may refer to Leith's 6-pounders, and not to some other battery which was present previously, but if the reader will refer to Napier's third volume of *The Peninsular War*, Appendix, he will find Reynier

COMMANDING THE ARTILLERY, BRIG.-GEN. HAWORTH.

	Guns.	Position.
LT.-COL. FRAMINGHAM, R.H.A.		
I Troop R.H.A. (now I Battery R.H.A.) — 6-pr., Capt. Bull.	6	With Cole.
A Troop R.H.A. (Chestnut Troop, now (A) R.H.A.) — 6-pr., Capt. Ross, Lieut. Hew Lane.	6	With Craufurd.
LT.-COL. ROBE, R.A.		
King's German A., 4th Company — 6-pr., Capt. Cleeve.	6	Front of Porta da Sulla.
4th Regt. Portuguese Artillery — 6-pr., Capt. Passos.	6	Right of Cleeve.
Depôt 3rd Brigade R.A., or No. 7 of 8th Batt. R.A., or 87th Batt. R.F.A., or No. 1 of 2nd Depôt Division R.A. — 9-pr., Capt. Lawson, Lieut. W. B. Ingleby,* Mr. Causton.	6	1/9-pr. and 1 Howitzer with Pack, 4/9-pr., high plateau.
MAJOR HARTMAN, K.G.A.		
K.G.A., 2nd Company — 6-pr., Capt. Retberg.	6	High plateau.
D4 R.A., or No 6 of 7th Batt. R.A. (now D Batt. 11th Brig. R.A., or 18th Batt. R.F.A.) — 6-pr., Capt. Thompson, 2nd Capt. H. B. Lane, Lieut. F. Bayley.	6	2 guns on knoll commanding ravine in Merle's attack and 4 guns nearer Lightburne.
MAJOR VON ARENTSCHILDT, K.G.A.		
2 guns brought by Major Dickson to Pass	2	Pass of S. Antonio.
1 Battery Portuguese Artillery — 6-pr., Capt. Rossieres (or) Preto.	6	One on high central plateau and the other above "funnel ravine" on right of Passos's Battery.†
1 ,, ,, — 3-pr., Capts. de Sylva or Freire.		
1 ,, ,, — 3-pr., ,, ,,	6	At the Pass.
1 ,, ,, — 9-pr.	6	At the Pass.
1 ,, ,, (Leith's) — 6-pr.	4	
MAJOR DICKSON (HILL'S ARMY CORPS).		
1 Battery Portuguese Artillery — 6-pr., Capt. Pedro da Rossieres.	10	Unable to get to the Pass in time for the battle, except 2 guns.
1 ,, ,, — 6-pr., Capt. João da Cunha Preto.		
Total present, 13 batteries	= 76	
Deduct 10, unable to get up	= 10	
In action	66 guns : but vide page 137.	

* Died as Sir William Ingleby, K.C.B., Col.-Commandant R.A.   † Not known which battery was in these two positions.

147

wrote to Masséna at 8 a.m. on the 26th September, that there were then six guns at the Pass of S. Antonio, and we know that Major Von Arentschildt passed Lightburne's Brigade at daylight on the 27th September, taking with him to the Pass another battery; so it appears to be established that he commenced the action with twelve guns at the Pass, and ended with eighteen guns, of which two were dismounted by the enemy's artillery.

It may also be noted that Picton, in his letter of the 3rd November, 1810, to Colonel Pleydel, states:

> On the evening of the 26th I detached the 88th Regiment nearly a mile to the left of the Pass of S. Antonio, etc. The 74th Regiment and the two Portuguese battalions, with twelve pieces of cannon, were stationed for the immediate defence of the Pass, and the 45th Regiment was kept in reserve.

This confirms the other authorities, Beresford and Burgoyne, and Duncan has followed them.

CHAPTER 13

After the Battle

When Masséna found the position of the Allies could not be carried by force, he held a consultation with certain of his generals, and thereafter decided to turn the position, if possible. Next day he learnt that this could be done by a road which passed round Wellington's left, *via* the Boialva Pass and Sardao.

He ordered demonstrations to be made against the Allies, under cover of which the French Army was withdrawn on the 28th September towards the pass.

Wellington, however, noticed that defensive works were being thrown up by the French, and that their troops were being withdrawn gradually. He also discerned French Cavalry moving at a great distance towards Mortagua, and drew the conclusion that Masséna probably intended using the Boialva Pass for a turning movement.

He still acted with great caution, and, whilst setting his troops in motion for a retreat, he took steps to thwart Masséna in the event of the true movement being towards the right of the Allies. On the night of the 28th most of his troops were, however, in full retreat by two routes, *i.e. via* Coimbra, Pombal, and Leiria, and *via* Espinhal and Thomar, towards the lines of Torres Vedras.

On the 29th only Craufurd's rear-guard was left at the convent, while the cavalry were patrolling towards the late position of the French.

Even these were, however, withdrawn during the day.

A considerable quantity of gunpowder was not removed by the Allies, but was blown up during the night of the 28th near the Porta da Rainha, while at Coimbra considerable stores of provisions were destroyed before the town was abandoned. The inhabitants, who had not left their houses, in accordance with the Proclamation of the Portuguese Government, were now made to do so, and flocked to Lisbon by all the roads.

What occurred at the convent after the battle will be found well told in Fr. Jose's *Diary*—in the next chapter.

The Battle of Bussaco was the real turning point of the war, and its consequences were more important than has been generally acknowledged by historians. The whole course of after events was influenced by this victory—and the moral effect in England and on the Continent was very great—especially in connection with the subsequent capture of Masséna's hospitals by Trant, and the hopeless situation into which Masséna soon drifted before the lines of Torres Vedras. It was the first of a string of disasters which culminated in the French being driven out of Portugal, as a ruined and demoralised army, under a discredited general.

"Busaco."—The following regiments bear on their roll of honour this battle name, *viz*.:—

Per 3rd batt.,	1st foot,	The Royal Scots (Lothian Regiment).
„ 2nd „	5th „	The Northumberland Fusiliers
„ 1st „	9th „	The Norfolk Regiment.
„ 2nd „	38th „	The South Staffordshire Regiment.
„ 1st „	43rd „	The Oxfordshire and Buckinghamshire
„ 1st „	52nd „	Light Infantry.
„ 1st „	45th „	The Sherwood Foresters.
„ 1st „	74th „	The Highland Light Infantry.
„ 2nd „	83rd „	The Royal Irish Rifles
„ 1st „	88th „	The Connaught Rangers.
„ 5th „	60th rifles,	The King's Own Rifle Corps.
„ —	95th „	The Rifle Brigade (Prince Consort's Own).

It seems strange that the Royal Fusiliers and the Queen's Own Cameron Highlanders do not bear it.

★★★★★★

N.B. List of regiments bearing "Busaco" upon their colours or appointments added since the book was first printed:

The Royal Fusiliers (City of London Regiment), per the 1st and 2nd battalions 7th Foot.

The South Wales Borderers, per the 2nd battalion 24th Foot.

The Gloucestershire Regiment, per the 28th Foot and 61st Foot.

The Black Watch (Royal Highlanders), per the 2nd battalion 42nd Foot.

The Queen's Own Cameron Highlanders, per the 1st battalion 79th Foot.

★★★★★★

CHAPTER 14

Bussaco Convent

Diary of the events observed in the Convent of Bussaco in the months of September and October, 1810, on the occasion of the French war, written by Brother Jose de S. Silvestre, a recluse, of the same convent, who was the witness of it all.

After the great disaster at the fortress of Almeida which was well known to all Portugal, on the 31st of August, 1810, the French Army, under the command of Prince d'Essling, Masséna, continued its march on Vizeu. The Anglo-luso Army, commanded by the English general, Lord Wellington, that was encamped in the folds of the Serra da Estrella, not being able to stop the march of the French, was directed by him on Ponte da Murcella, and so rapidly that nothing was known here of the march until the troops arrived here, which happened on the 19th day of September of the said year of 1810.

The great height of this Serra gave cause to the successful occurrences that I shall now relate.

20th day of September.—At 1, at night, there arrived here an *aide-de-camp* of Lord Wellington; when we opened the gate he said he wished to see the convent, crying:"Now! now! as by 2 p.m. tomorrow the general-in-chief will be here. He sleeps this night at Lorvao; the French have already reached Tondella."

A communication was at once made to the abbot, who showed him the convent and the Chapel of the Bishop. He ordered us to have the best room whitewashed and cleaned for the general; and after drinking a little wine the *aide-de-camp* hurried off to Lorvao. Orders were given to prepare the lodging, and our day ended in fear, for we now saw ourselves obliged to tolerate things never before known in this house.

151

This shows the entrance of the Convent as it was at the time of Wellington's visit. He slept in a tiny room behind the small cross on the wall. He had another small room for his office, and there were two ways of leaving the Convent open to him—one by the office door and the other by the Convent door.

21st day.—Being assured of the march of the French, this morning the abbot ordered us to consume the Holy Sacrament, in order that this great God, whom we adore by day and night, might not suffer any irreverence.

By 8 a.m. there arrived here the quarter-master-general; he gave us a roll of the officers to whom we must give quarters; there were fifty. He gave it signed by the general-in-chief, and it declared that we were only to give accommodation to those for whom it was so ordered.

Afterwards the English soldiers began to appear, and outside they increased so much that by 9 o'clock all the wood was full; and the convent and the hermitage were also full of English officers and their baggage.

The general entered at the same hour into the convent; we showed him his room; it did not please him, in spite of it being the best, because it had only one door. He chose another more secure, for it had two. He ordered us to wash the place, and to dry it by lighting a fire. While this was being done, he went to look at all the Serra, and the roads towards Mortagua.

All the cells were occupied by the officers of the staff corps, except that of the Father Prior, Brother Antonio of the Angels, which nobody wanted, because it was found full of lumber, rags, and old iron, nor that of the abbot, which was politely reserved for him.

The monks, during all the time that the troops were there, slept in the church, the Sacristy, the house opposite, the library, and dispensary, or wherever they could find room. As soon as Lord Wellington came in, he broke up the confinement for all kinds of persons, which had never been done since the foundation (of the convent).

The general desired that the bells should not be rung at night. For this reason, we held matins at 8 p.m.

Now, late at night, there arrived here a *"religioso,"* a Spaniard of Escurial, entirely disguised, to whom we gave shelter. He told us, that if the French came, we should not stay here, because in Spain, where the general's quarters were, they brought much ruin, and caused many deaths.

22nd day.—This day the troops continued to fill up the Serra. The general, all the time he was here, rose before 5 a.m., by 7 a.m. he went to see the camp and the army, and at 4 p.m. he came back, and by 5 p.m. he dined. He ordered that we should be quiet, and said that he would warn us when we ought to go away.

A Barefooted Carmelite.

But the abbot, being more cautious, ordered the oldest brothers to depart, and the cart carried the valuables of the convent to Coimbra, and he sent immediately a communication from himself to our Father-General.

23rd day.—At midday much attention began to be paid to great firing in Mortagua, which announced the vicinity of the enemy; it continued all the evening; at the same time many houses were observed to be burning in the neighbourhood of that town.

The English officers went out at once to watch it from the Porta Sulla—evincing great sadness at the sight. The inhabitants of the neighbourhood, oppressed by the troops, and afraid of the enemy, immediately left their houses and fled for this Serra, and many found an asylum amongst us.

24th day.—The firing continued, in the districts round Mortagua, between our troops and the enemy—it had hardly any effect, as there were only engaged in it the advance guards on each side—theirs advancing as our people retired.

This day Lord Wellington gave an order to open the Gate of Rainha, that was closed with stones—so as to be nearer to the Serra in the direction of Murcella (*i.e.* by the main road). From this point our peasants began to open a great road all along the crest of the Serra in the direction of Murcella, and made another within the enclosure to pass the troops and artillery along the crest.

The soldiers also opened the other corner of the wall at the top of the wood, to take wood to burn, and for building huts.

25th day.—This morning the French advanced upon our troops near Moura, a village distant from here a quarter of a league. They stopped there, spreading out their columns on all the heights on both flanks.

Our army was at once placed in a line all along the crest of the Serra, of which this wood was the centre. Batteries were immediately made throughout the mountains.

Near the Porta Sulla, within the wall, they also made one with a view of attacking the enemy entering by the gate. Almost all the wall that looked to the east on both the sides of that gate was thrown down from the middle to the top, and loopholed below.

Behind it were posted two regiments, more easily to attack the French if they got there.

Nearly all round the same gate outside there was also constructed

The two iron bell-stands on the Convent tower. One of the bells which Wellington ordered not to be rung at night is visible, also the old clock tower and the top of the other bell-stand.

a great oak stockade, in order that we might succeed in repulsing the enemy. All this was made no use of.

Some of our regiments who had been near the firs of Moura, returned tonight to the Serra, leaving unoccupied the two villages, Moura and Sulla, which were too near to the enemy.

The regular life of the convent was suspended on account of the many interruptions.

26th day.—As soon as he got up, the general ordered all his baggage to be taken out of the wood.

This caused us great dread, so much so that some prepared themselves for flight.

By noon the baggage came back again to the convent; then he ordered dinner to be made, much to our relief.

Our army reinforced the line it had already taken up.

The French, who had occupied in great numbers the mountains in front, were seen steadily drawing nearer to us. One column entered Moura, and many others posted themselves in the neighbouring fir plantations in the valleys. At 2 p.m. our artillery began to play on them. The *caçadores* descended the mountain and did the same, and their fire lasted with but little effect until 4 p.m.

An English general was mortally wounded (see note), and he was carried to the Chapel of the Bishop. Lord Wellington, on the day following, ordered us to find a skiff (?) for this wounded man; it was not given him because we had none. We were suspicious that he had died, or that he was so ill that only thus would he be able to go to Coimbra.

27th day.—Today the general got up very early. He at once ordered his baggage to be taken outside the Wood. From 4 or 5 in the morning the French took advantage of a thick fog; having in the night climbed up through all the valleys which intervened between the two armies, they advanced with great impetuosity against our troops, principally on the two roads which go from Mortagua to Coimbra.

As the fog concealed the nearness of the French on the road of Sancta Antonio do Cantaro, they approached intending to break our line; it was an unfortunate attempt for them, as all those who reached the crest of the Serra did not get back again, because a regiment of ours assisting quickly to close the line, some were killed, and most of the others taken prisoners.

On the other road they did not get so far; but still they entered Sulla, and reached the nearest of our artillery.

This at once began to play upon them with all its force, and the *caçadores* did the same.

The mist shortly afterwards lifted, and then were discovered the great multitude of French who had reached that point. As the fire of our artillery was very lively, and theirs could play scarcely at all, a great part of that column fled rapidly down the mountain. Our *caçadores* greeted them at the same time with a great hooting, which gave great joy to those who heard and observed the occurrence. The fire lasted from side to side with great effect and activity till 4 p.m.

At 8 a.m., after I and the other *padre* had confessed and said Mass, I went out of the convent to see the fight, entering by the gate that is at the foot of the tank. I encountered there a peasant lamenting; I asked him what was the matter. He answered me, almost without pronouncing a word clearly, "Do you not see that?"

"Oh, what?" said I.

He explained, "Some wounded French that are there."

I repaired at once below, where I saw the most miserable people, so much so that, without wishing it, my tears at once began to fall.

One of them, that caused most tenderness, had his face traversed from one side to the other by a ball that was now in his chin, the blood ran out by his mouth, and he had already a great deal of it coagulated below his two lips. He nevertheless was not able to speak a word. The others were not so bad, except four or five that were wounded in the middle, and so much drained of blood that they trembled with cold. The English made quickly a great bonfire round them. I went away quickly from there because I could not see with equanimity such pitiable things.

I climbed to the top of the wood; on the outside of the gate, that had been there opened, were the surgeons binding the wounded of our *caçadores*, who were many, but none so badly wounded and pitiable as the French.

I continued my walk by the Serra outside, to see if I could see the fight; it was not possible for me, for the balls of the enemy reached the crest of the Serra on that side. I went to the middle of the wood. The fire obliged our regiments that were not engaged to lie down, somewhat below the height.

As I could not see the fight I returned to the house. When I arrived, a soldier of the general's guard told me that there was a prisoner, a French general named Simon. I went at once to see him. He was wounded with three balls, all in the face.

View from the Cruz Alto towards the north. The Cruz Alto was on the position used in old days as a "look-out" station, and was on the hillside above the Convent. Wellington would no doubt have a watch kept from there. The Carmelites would pass this way when climbing the hill to see the fight.

A captain also came with him, who served as his secretary (*aide-de-camp*), but he was not wounded.

Lord Wellington ordered him to be treated with all honour and humanity, and an English officer gave him his room. Lord Wellington ordered his baggage to be sent for.

Masséna sent it promptly. His wife came also; all this by the following morning.

The abbot ordered us to consecrate a piece of ground in the olive-grove, in which to inter the wounded who had died.

Our *caçadores* endured much today, because they had not at any time wavered; in fact, they sustained with great animation and valour the combat all day.

One of their captains told me at night, that they had had three days like this, and that only one *caçadore* had escaped. As a matter of fact, the dead were not many, but the wounded were numerous. Those only that were in the courtyard, where they were brought, since the binding of their wounds, went away in eighty carriages, at night, to Botao. To all of them we gave wine, and other things for which they asked.

One thing we extracted from many of them; that being about to die, some at the foot of others, and all of them in great peril of life, none sought confession, nor were yet heard to call on Jesus, which is so proper and natural in an afflicted Christian.

Beresford, who had his quarters in Sancta Euphemia, came this night to sleep at our library.

28th day.—As soon as it was morning the general ordered the retreat of his baggage as on the previous days.

The French general, who was a prisoner, went to Coimbra with his wife and secretary.

Our artillery continued to fire upon the enemy—but that of the French played little, or not at all, upon us. There was little blood shed this day. The French set on fire the woods on the mountains at dark.

Trant came today to speak with Lord Wellington; a rumour at once arose that some regiments were to go with him. This commandant went by evening to Agueda, where he had some militia.

At 11 p.m. the French were very still, turning their faces from Ponte da Murcella, they drew back to Mortagua. From there, marching by the road of Boialvo, they went as though to place themselves in Porto, that point being without any protection.

An English officer that was on the look-out, and who by good chance (by reason of the darkness of the night) noticed the movement of the enemy, at once told the general.

He got up immediately, and by the middle of the night left for Coimbra with all the army.

He ordered his people to advise us to retire also, which all did, except the *padre* fr. Antonio da Soledade, the brother fr. Ignacio da Nativedade, and me. We did not go out, for it was very dark and raining.

We had the intention of marching in the morning, trusting that there must remain in the Serra some provisions, and that the French would not enter here at night.

29th day.—I got up early in the morning to observe the movements of the troops; I met in the yard many regiments marching precipitately. I asked if there remained any people on the Serra—they answered that they had left none. With this notice we were alarmed.

I allowed them to pass, and I went again outside the Porta Sulla to look at the camp of the French. There appeared now only some pickets of cavalry spread out on all the roads. The nearest soon began to move, and they went retiring each lot alternately, until they all disappeared. A battalion of English cavalry who were in observation soon sent a picket to watch the road to Mortagua. They came across near Moura seventy wounded Frenchmen, forsaken entirely, in a mass. They pitied them so much that they dismounted, and mounted them on their horses, and brought them to the Chapel of the Almas, that was on the outside of the wall. They spent all this day in this work of piety.

At night we made out the fires of the enemy by the parts of Agueda.

The English soon fired a great lot of powder near the wall on the lower side of the Porta da Rainha. It did us great damage. It threw to the ground the wall that was in front of it, dragged out some trees, and broke a large and excellent glass window of the church, with its window-sashes.

30th day.—Today, in the morning, the English soldiers that were sentinels went away.

They recommended us to give water to the wounded that were in the Chapel of Almas, that we should deliver them to the country people, and that they should not rob and kill, and we should order them to seek the few others who were deserted in the Serra.

At 9 a.m. I asked two Portuguese officers who were here to accompany me to see the wounded that remained on the mountain; they went promptly; but coming near the Porta Sulla they left me

The Porta da Sulla. Traces remain of the partial demolition of the wall for defence ; the holes into which poles were inserted to carry the planking on which the defenders were posted can be seen. A favourite amusement at Bussaco is now donkey riding, and a family is here to be seen out for the daily ride.

alone, saying that it was too far, that they would not go there.

I marched as far as Moira; met in that place three men, and said to them, "Would you accompany me?" They went at once.

We followed the road; near it we soon found twelve wounded men full of much misery, so bad that only one could rise; they seemed to have broken legs, and three were almost dead, through pains, cold, heat, hunger, and thirst. After they saw me, they raised their hands to Heaven, and lamented much, and said with loud voices, "Oh! Mother of God! Oh! Mother of God! Water, water, for the love of God." After conversing with a few of them, I told the peasants who had been with me, to go and seek water for them; they answered me that they would not do it; that it was not incumbent on them to do good to their enemies. I, pitying to see the inhumanity of those hearts, made every effort to move them to compassion.

I said to them that these wounded men were not now our enemies; that they had been so before, but they were not able now to do evil to anybody—I said that they themselves might someday be in the same state, and in the same misery, banished from their lands, without the protection of their country, deserted by friends and acquaintances of the same nation, abandoned by all human help, delivered to the rigour of the sun, of cold, of famine, and of thirst—without being able to walk a step to procure any subsistence. If they fell into the same misfortune as they saw these miserable ones to be in, what would they desire? What would they wish should be done to them? Let us, then, do to them as we should wish them to do to us. We ought to love our neighbour, and even our enemies, so ordered Jesus Christ—and the Holy Church for the same reason.

This makes a good Christian, and he that wishes to go to heaven, ought to do all that I have told you.

In spite of all this, my exhortation, they did not at once move. I said to them at last that if they did not wish to go and seek water for the sick, I myself would search for it.

I at once took some few bottles and other vessels that were there, and went to a neighbouring valley below.

Seeing my promptness, the peasants were then moved to pity, and one of them went with me; he asked me with great urgency to permit him to carry the water, but I did not wish to give him more than one of the vessels. I arrived with the water and portioned it out for all, and one peasant even gave them a bit of bread that he drew out of the pocket of his jacket. These wounded had not eaten anything but some

The Capella das Almas and Portuguese guard-house on the road from the Porta da Rainha to the Monumento.

This is the road from the Convent to the Capella, along which the French officers would go when making their visit to the wounded.

ears of maize that were near them.

I wished to bring away one that had not wounds in his legs; I told him to lean on me; I helped him to rise, but he was so drained of blood from a great wound, that he was light-headed, and very weak, so that, after being supported, he could not walk a step; he soon fell on the ground insensible.

As I could not bring anyone, I went to the convent, bringing with me three bottles to carry water. After midday I carried them there, also some bread, wine, and fish.

I brought them in a barrow as far as near Moura, in which a poor old man from Lobao helped me. We could not draw them any further because we were incapacitated by so much toil.

I recommended much to the inhabitants of this place who then arrived, that they should give water to the wounded, and that they should seek for any others that might be about there, and this they did for four days, coerced by my continual urgency.

Already three of the wounded had died owing to the cold of the night, and the great heat of the day, and of their own miseries.

I helped to put the rest in a dwelling full of straw, where we continued to treat them with all humanity, giving them every day bread, wine, and fish, while the people of the place gave them water—until we brought them to the Chapel of the Almas, where the others were, and to all we gave daily the necessary subsistence. Near night there came to us notice of the arrival of the French at Mealhada.

1st day of October.—Early in the morning a rumour was current here that the French were at Vaçarica, a place distant from here a quarter of a league to the west. This caused us great dread.

The father who had remained with me, told me that he did not know how to get rid of the two officers above mentioned. They were a captain of Ordenança and a lieutenant of *caçadores*, who had already been eight days here, having introduced themselves with an air of friendship, and whom we were keeping. I said to him, "Do you know the way to do, without doing wrong? As the French are already at Vaçarica, let us pass the word that we wish to shut the convent and fly, so as not to fall into their hands—then let us go as far as the Serra, and when we like we will return."

He approved of my suggestion, because we were now cautious; we had no intention of leaving the convent, because as soon as we turned our backs, the people of the neighbouring villages (who were all hid-

165

The village of Moira, or Moura, from which the French wounded were brought to the Capella das Almas do Encarnadouro. Moira was where Masséna was stationed during the battle, and from near that village Loison's and Marchand's Divisions commenced their advance to the attack.

den in the Wood) would at once come and rob us of all, which would perhaps be worse than the French would do.

I went at once to the said officers, I told them to remove all they had there; that we wished to shut the convent, and that no one was to stay within the gates.

They, who did not wish to go, began to say that the French were not come there, and that they were not even at Vaçarica, and that the youth who had brought such news ought to be given the stick.

I answered them that without delay they must prepare themselves, as infallibly we had to close the convent and decamp.

When our young men heard this, they said that they would not go, because they had kneaded bread, and could not leave it. I told them then, in secret, my determination, which they applauded, because they also were disgusted with the two officers, for they had seen them collect much powder and muskets that were found in the wood, and on the field of battle; and they were eating and drinking at our cost.

Then, taking the men by the coats, they urged much that they should go quickly.

The said persons said to me that they had to breakfast first. I answered them, "There is not now time for so much, drink a pint and no more; we go out from here without more delay."

Accordingly, they prepared an old horse, that had remained in the Wood, to carry what they had collected. I went to the cellar to drink a pint of wine. At this time, I perceived there, outside, a troop of cavalry. I locked the door quickly, and said to the others that were preparing themselves, "What cavalry is this that comes here?" I went then to the gate of the yard, and saw some few cavalry soldiers marching slowly below. At first sight they seemed to be English, but, noticing soon their head-dress, I knew them to be French.

Seeing them then from within, I said to the others, "Were not they telling me that the French were not coming here? They are here already"—and I pointed them out at the same time with my hand, again returning myself to the outside.

The French continued their slow march without saying anything to me, at which I wondered, and I concluded that they did not wish to speak to me; only they called to a youth that was flying, that he should stop and not fly, which he did.

In the middle of them came three officers. As soon as they saw me, beckoning me with the hand, they said, "Come here, sir."

I went then promptly. One of them, as soon as I arrived, taking

167

off his helmet, saluted me, with much politeness, in the Portuguese fashion. That done, he put his helmet on his head, and said to me: "We come to take account of the magazines of provisions that the English have left here."

I answered, "The English have left here nothing more than much powder, which they burnt when they left."

They added, "At what hour was this fire?"

I told them, "It was at night."

They smiled then, because they saw that I had spoken the truth, since they had heard a great noise at that time. They asked me also if there were any troops in the wood.

"No, gentlemen."

"How many monks are there here?" I told them, "Only three, most fled, according to the order received from the English general."

They again insisted that there were magazines of provisions here— as they had said. I answered that there was nothing of the kind— that they had been deceived. They replied, "Tomorrow there will be here another French officer to learn whether it is true or not."

This word caused me much fear. I said to them then, "Sir Officer, dismount, and I will show you the whole convent."

He remained much contented, and told me to have no fear, that he would be quiet, that they would do no mischief, that they would give a paper in order that nobody should do evil.

The other father came now to me with the two persons that we wished to depart outside. The lieutenant was at once made a prisoner for being with belt and sword; then the officers, after they saw him, said, "You must come with us, keep on your belt and your sword."

To the other officer this did not happen at once, because he walked without uniform, and pulled off, without their seeing him, the galloon of his hat, but it occurred afterwards, as I will recount later on. They asked if we had any corn, any wine, and baked bread.

I answered them, "The bread is kneaded for baking, there is some corn and wine."

"Was there much?" say they.

"I would show it them," I replied. I showed them all that. The corn was of Coimbra, because I could not show them our own, it being all placed in a great tun.

They asked for bags, and ordered two peasants to go and carry about seven or eight *alqueires*, a great pot of wine, a canister of millet-bread, and fifty codfish for the soldiers whom they left with the wounded at the Chapel of Almas; then to the convent came only the officers and ten or twelve soldiers, so that there should be no wasting and nobody insulted—according to what they had said.

That done, one of the officers, seeing a large butt in the gate of the buttery, asked that it should be opened with all speed, thinking that there was hidden there some great thing.

As soon as he entered, he cast his eyes on a canister of mackerel very well salted. He asked what fish was that. He gave some to the soldier that was there, and ordered him to cook some as quickly as possible for the officers.

I told him that they were very salt, that without being first sweetened they would not be of use.

He answered that that did not matter, that he would order to cook, "quickly, quickly."

To this matter went all his attention, and without seeing anything more they went outside, and told me that they would come up to the Hall. I conducted them to the Refectory. As soon as we arrived there, they asked that they should go to eat. I told them that the food was not yet ready, that they should wait to dine; to which they answered that they could not delay, because they had to enter Coimbra by the middle of the day jointly with the general—that they would have all badly cooked "like the English."

We gave them millet-bread, because we had not other bread baked, wine, eggs, fruit, and the said salt mackerel—and with that they remained content. Being at table, they asked for port wine, cheese, and sweets. We told them that we had not any of these. They assented.

At this time there came a soldier to give them information that the peasants were walking armed outside the walls. They ordered me that I should arrange with them that they should leave their arms, that they should not do ill, that they should occupy their houses and cultivate the fields; that war was for soldiers and not for them.

I asked that they should order a soldier to go with me, which they did promptly.

When I arrived at the Porta da Rainha, the soldier did not wish that I should go further; he went alone to speak to the others, who were at the Chapel of Almas. He came back quickly, and told me that there was nothing the matter, and we returned to the convent.

The case was this: there came a *clerico* to speak with us; he brought a musket on his back. When he arrived at the gate the soldiers cried to him from above that he should abandon the arm; he, thinking they were English, did not do so.

A youth, who was at the gate, told him at once that he should leave the musket, and come, that they would not do him harm. He asked, "What soldiers are they?"

"They are French."

As soon as he heard this, he decamped in an open carriage down the hill.

As soon as they saw him fly, a soldier went after him, and discharged a pistol, but without a bullet.

Asked afterwards why he ran with such haste, he answered that he feared they would rob him of his money, because he had no more than he carried with him.

When we arrived at the convent, I asked the soldier to go and give a report to the officers; he asked me to give him a little wine in a bottle.

I told the other *padre* that he might give it him, but as soon as he opened the door of the cellar, all the others went also with them to ask wine; he, being vexed that there were so many, and much wine being spilt, told me that I should satisfy them.

I ordered them all to go out; they did not wish to do so without filling well their bottles. As they did not desire to obey, I told a youth, with an angry voice, to go and call an officer to put out these soldiers.

As soon as they heard that they began to go out very sad; the captain came soon, and put them out in an instant; they did not speak more about wine.

I then locked the door—after that they asked for some fowls; they took four fowls and two partridges.

They urged us much that we should give the wounded bread, wine, and broth, that we should arrange with the peasants, that one should sleep there. The lay brother went to sleep there, and also a youth, two nights. The lay brother did not go again, because the wounded said that it sufficed if the youth went.

When the officers went out to the yard to march, a soldier told them that there were in one of the servants' rooms muskets and powder. He went within at once, broke six muskets, put outside a barrel of powder, and threw the cartridges into a bowl of water that was there. In order to draw out the bowl from under a bed it was necessary for him to take off his gun, which he was carrying on his back, and this he forgot to take with him in his haste to leave. The gun remained in payment for those he had broken. When they were about to march, they heard a youth say that the said person that was without uniform was a captain. Directly they heard that they said to him, "Are you an officer? If so, put on your sword and your belt." He was embarrassed and did not know what to answer. We told them that he was certainly a captain, but of the Ordenança, that there was none of it there, that it was far off. As soon as we gave them this excuse, they did not urge more. But they said to him, that he had to come with them. He made great solicitations not to go, he told them that he was the cousin of my companion, arriving at the same time as he, and that he was not able to leave—but the father answered him, "Go, go, and do the will of these gentlemen."

Hearing this, they made him march with them, and also the other that they had also taken prisoner when he fled.

I asked them to give me the paper they had promised; they asked ink and paper, and gave me the writing as follows:

(In French.)

In the name of humanity, I pray and supplicate all French military men who come to the Convent of Bussaco to exact nothing from the fathers, nor from the peasants of the neighbouring villages; 60 wounded French will be the victims of the least violence. These fathers are obliged to furnish provisions to the wounded up to the moment of departure.

The 4th October, 1810.

.... Officer of the 3rd Regt. of Hussars.

In Portuguese that is to say:

Em nome da humanidade,

Eu rogo e supplico a todos os militares francezes que vierem ao convento do Bussaco de nao exigerem nada, nem dos padres, nem dos paizanos das aldeas vizinhos: 60 feridos francezes seriam victimas da menor violencia. Estes padres se obrigaram a dar viveres aos feridos ate o momento da evacuaçao.

They asked me also for a certificate to show to the general as to how we had saved the wounded. I passed it to him in the following form:

Fr. José and the other *religiosos* of the Convent of Bussaco certify to *Messieurs* the Officers of the French Army in Portugal that, since the departure of the English troops, we have taken care of, and continue to take care of, the 60 French wounded

171

that remained on the field, giving them bread, wine, and cod-fish, for we have not anything else.

F. I. S. S.

Bussaco, *1 de Outubro de* 1810.

They told us that the day following there would come another picket; they dismissed themselves with the same Portuguese polite-ness as when they entered, and marched by the same road as they had come by, carrying at their side, and on foot, the two prisoners.

These French did not ask money, nor did they give us the least in-sult, in spite of encountering here many peasants, armed with powder and ball.

2nd day.—At 8 or 9 a.m. there entered by the lower gate a picket of fifty French, and it was travelling by the convent.

I was at the gate of the yard, when they arrived very quietly. I was going to the first soldier to show him the paper that had been given me the day before, and he, seeing me put my hand in my pocket, said, "Money! Money!" I drew the paper out, and as soon as he saw it he did not ask more for money—he ordered me to go to the officers who were in the centre of the picket, and were now moving to the front.

The officers, as soon as they saw me with the paper in my hand, called me to them. I delivered to them the said paper.

One after that spoke with the others, and delivered it to me, saying at once not to have any fear—that they would be tranquil and quiet, and do no ill; that they came to take a roll of the wounded, that they might be conducted to hospital.

They dismounted, placed guards at the bottom of the yard, and the same at the convent gate, and without entering within, asked that I should show them the wounded. They went on foot, conversing with me; there were a captain, a lieutenant, an ensign, and a Spanish doctor.

After they saw the wounded, the doctor told me to order warm water to bathe their wounds. I came with him to the convent with that end. When I arrived, the lay brother came to me, very pale, and told me that the soldiers had made great waste in the church, and had also torn his waistcoat feeling for money. "What good has your paper brought?" he asked.

These were the facts: as soon as the officers went to see the wounded, some few soldiers breaking the principal gate of the con-vent (which had been without guards, as it was not seen by the offic-ers) went to the Chapel of the Lord, "*Ecce homo*," broke the door of a recess that was there, threw down the niche of "Little Jesus," breaking the glass that was in front; they entered the church, broke the gate of the recess, smashed the glass of the "Little Jesus" that is in the Chapel of the "Lady of Leite," but they did not break that, though they stole a dress of Christ that it had at the neck; they cut some cords with which the church was furnished, and, the sacristan being at the gate by the church, they did not enter there, and so there escaped there a chalice with which we say Mass; they went to the cell of the prior by the window, and they broke into chips the chest of three keys. My companion, who heard this tumult, ran to see who it was; he met two soldiers at the entrance to the gate of the "house opposite" where we slept. He called to them from the top of the dormitory, "What is the matter? Oh, comrades!"

They answered, "Wine, wine." He told them then to come and he would give them wine. They came at once, and he, in place of taking them to the cellar, put them in the middle of the others who were in the yard. He told a sergeant who was there that the officers had promised not to do ill to the convent, and that the soldiers had spoilt all.

He at once drew his sword, and went with him inside the convent to put them out. When they were passing the gate of the store of firewood, they met these two men grasping the said lay brother to pillage him, but the said sergeant separated them at once.

I showed all this damage to the doctor, and then when the said officers arrived, I said to the captain, "Sir, the soldiers entered the convent, tore the waistcoat of a brother, and have done much damage, and I am going to show it to you." Taking him at the same time by the arm, I went to show him. They were all very sad.

Going out to the yard, they told nothing of what they went to see; they asked if we knew the soldiers. I told them that my companion did not, but that there was a sergeant that had put them out; he knew well who they were.

They called out for him, and ordered him to go and seek the accomplices in the crime; he went in an instant, and brought three soldiers before him, without head-dress, without arms, and without belts, and one had his face running with blood.

The officers, without saying anything to them, went to show them what they had done at the gate of the recess. One of them, beginning at once to deny it, the lieutenant, grasping him by the coat collar, beat him on the back, by the steps of the great altar. Entering then another to deny it, the ensign laid into him with a plank of chestnut, and gave him so much, and such great blows on his back, that I, fearing there any blood, took him by the arms and told him not to give any more. He complied. The third said nothing, and thus escaped, but he was very pale.

An officer, coming to me with his helmet in hand, said to me, "Have they robbed the Holy Sacrament?"

"No, sir, because we had taken precautions; they broke only the gate."

After this they went out to the yard, they commenced to give us much comfort, said that they had not known of that door, so that they had not posted sentries as they had done at the others; they ordered four soldiers there at once, and suggested that we should write to the general, that he would give us satisfaction, and that this convent would be always respected.

Speaking quietly, showing in the face much sentiment, the captain, coming near me, asked me these formal words, "if by favour I could give the officers only bread and wine?"

"Yes, sir. How many are there?"

"Four," answered he.

I went within; taking the captain by the arm, I brought him to the refectory. We gave them bread, wine, and codfish; they asked cheese and sweets, but as soon as we told them we had none, they acquiesced.

They asked also that we should give to their comrades, and to those who were on guard, a little bread and new wine, but to the others who had been bad, nothing.

I told them that we had no new wine, that we had old of that which they had been drinking; they replied, "It is bad expending such wine on a soldier."

They sent us an orderly that he might show and teach us who the soldiers were, because we did not know them. There were twelve; to these we gave that which the officers had said.

After the castigation of the delinquents, they behaved themselves well; in fact, they did not speak a single word. They all went to sleep in the middle of the yard—except the guards. When they were at table an officer told me that it was now four weeks since they had eaten bread, another said only three.

I asked what they ate. They answered that they ate grain of the same kind that they gave to the horses—and that they ground it with their teeth.

One asked me to give him some bread to carry. I gave him some, but he did not wish to accept it unless I gave him more. He took four loaves. To the other officers I gave one each, but these did not venture to ask for any.

When they went out from the table to go away, they found a peasant that had come to show them the way; he had cast himself down at the gate of the yard, and was groaning much.

I asked him what was the matter. Putting his hand to his breast, he said that he had a great affliction, and that he could not rise. I called to the doctor to see what was wrong. He felt his pulse, and told me to order a decoction of elder-flower.

He mounted then with the other officers, and all began to laugh because the man cried more and more. The doctor said then that it was a trick so that he might not accompany them. They asked me to order another peasant to show them the way. There went one that had been brought with a slash in his arm, promising us to let him go directly another should appear. This we did. They dismissed themselves politely from us, and marched by the height of the wood outside. After they had gone, the sick peasant got up from the ground, and without more moaning said, "Have these devils now gone? Much contempt they have shown me—let them go with Barabbas."

We, and the others that were there, began to laugh much; and he, improving all the time, disappeared from there without saying "*adieu*" to anybody.

3rd and 4th days. The French Army continued its march by Coimbra, and from there for Lisbon.

5th day. Today at 8 or 9 o'clock a peasant came to tell us to go to the Porta Sulla, that there were some of our soldiers there who wished to speak with us.

I told them, "This cannot be. Let them see that they are not French?"

He answered that he had spoken with them, that undoubtedly, they were ours. I went out much pleased, and said to him, "Proceed there, and show them to me."

When I went by the Chapel of Our Holy Mother Saint Theresa, I saw there five of the cavalry; and the sergeant brought a pistol in his hand, pointing it upwards; he entered thus into the convent and asked about the French. I told him that we had notice that they were at Botao—but below it.

After we had given him drink, and also the soldiers, he ordered me to speak with an ensign that had stayed with most of our soldiers at Moura; that he himself would go to see the wounded at the Chapel, and then go at once. I went there and also a youth. I gave the officer the information we had of the movements of the French; and with certainty that they were now not at Botao on the crest, distant from here a league.

He told me that I must go with him to give this report to the general, who was in Mortagua. I replied that I could not go, that he might give that report. He added that he would give me a beast, to go on horseback; that the general was very angry, and did not trust our officers, and always suspected what they said.

He sent the youth to the convent to seek a hat for himself, and a little bread and wine for the soldiers who had come.

As he was delaying much, I told the officer that he should excuse me going to Mortagua, that I would now go to the convent in order to see the bread and wine sent with all speed. It pained him much, but he agreed to my supplication. I came to the house and the youth went to deliver all; afterwards they left for Montagua, from there they followed the road of Boialvo, from whence had come the French.

Finally, in all the eight days that the quarter-master-general was here (the day of St. Matthew to the day of St. Miguel) there was no default in anything that they asked us. We gave beds to almost all the officers, all the cloths we had were apportioned out for them. For a general, that was in the Chapel of the Bishop, was given a table-cloth, two yellow candlesticks, a large copper water-pot, which served for water, and some napkins; all this was lost. For the Lord (Wellington) we gave the best napkins we had, four dozen candles, and all the rest of the things that the other officers were continually asking for. To the soldiers, and the people who came retreating, we gave salt and other things that we had.

We expended upon the troops much wine, much bread, much cheese, much butter, and other things in proportion. The Lord (Wellington) when he was leaving told the abbot that he wished to pay for what had been expended, and that the abbot should say how much he required. He answered, that he sought nothing but the peace of the kingdom.

This convent lost much by the troops; there disappeared almost all that we had given for the beds and tables of the officers, of which nothing was made good.

Besides the mischief done by the French, already above mentioned, we lost almost all the maize that was unripe; there was not more than two or three hogsheads of it; because they cut it for the beasts. We remained without beans, all the earth of the garden, that was sown with it, remained without any, because the soldiers and other people did not cease to gather whatever was seen by them.

The general ordered guards for it, but it was no good. There would be not less than forty or fifty *alqueires* of it.

The cabbages that were outside were also cut. We were deprived of all.

Many trees were spoilt, a great quantity of cedars which the abbot had ordered to be planted were almost all broken; the troops and all the people who came with them burnt as much wood as they liked, all through the forest.

The wall, which before had only two gates, one to the east and the other to the west, was left with six, all open—two on the crest, two at the bottom near to the road, and the two to the east and west broken open.

Beyond this: half the wall that looks to the east was thrown down from the middle to the top, as already referred to.

Finally, the door of the convent chapel was broken; they robbed us of a chalice that was there, a little oil, all the most precious adornment of the altar, and anything else that had any value.

On the retirement of the French for Spain, there came here to quarter himself with his troops the English commandant Wilson; on the two days that they were here we gave him all that he asked for his table and bed. To the soldiers also we gave much bread, and the rest that they asked if we were able to give it.

In spite of that they stole every orange that we had in our two orangeries; they went to the dispensary, broke the gate that goes out to the orangery, and stole all the bread they wanted, wine, a large basket of eggs, and a pan of honey, and many other things that pleased them, behaving the same as or worse than the French—and wherever they arrived they filled with desperation the minds of the villagers. These soldiers were not of the line; they were militia. They ought to have been better, but behaved worse than the others.

The Commandant Trant, after the taking of Coimbra, ordered the wounded that were left here to go to the Hospital of Oporto. In twenty days, that they remained here these wounded had nothing, but what we gave them, for subsistence.

As they were many, we gave them each a little, so as to supply to

The Capella das Almas, in which the seventy wounded French soldiers were sheltered for three weeks. The Portuguese guard-house is on the right.

all. If we had not done it, they would have all died of hunger and at the hands of the peasants.

Two peasants went there one day and robbed them of all that they had. They even took the shirts they were wearing. A *padre* went and found them in the greatest misery, without uniforms, without shirts, without trousers, and scarcely covered, with some rags and old robes. To such an extent was the inhumanity of a Portuguese possible; they were unworthy certainly of the name! Of these sixty wounded, there died twelve. I helped to take the dead out of the chapel, and the other *padre* helped to bury them. We sustained also an English sergeant, and a Hanoverian, that came to stay at the convent very sick, but not wounded.

To these we gave a bed at the foot of the refectory, and treated them with the greatest abundance, yet I was censured for that; but God gave me a heart that could not suffer inhumanity.

Before Lord Wellington came here the English had not entered here, in spite of passing this road continually by the crest and below. But since the battle the name of Bussaco, before unknown to many people, spread through all parts, made itself venerated, and the English officers who went or came to the army, came here to lodge, and were enchanted with this place.

There did not pass any week that some did not sleep here. We supplied them with all that they required, for themselves, as well as for their saddle beasts. We did the same for the Portuguese and the soldiers who passed here.

This put us to great expense; but to the end that there might come to us the peace so much desired, and so necessary as even life, we gave all for a good use.

Oh, that the Great God of Armies may see fit to grant it in a short time for His glory, and our joy!

INSCRIPTION FOR THE DESERTO DE BUSACO.

Reader! thou standest upon holy ground,
Which Penitence hath chosen for itself,
And war, disturbing the deep solitude,
Hath left it doubly sacred. On these heights
The host of Portugal and England stood,
Arrayed against Masséna, when the chief,
Proud of Rodrigo and Almeida won,
Pressed forward, thinking the devoted realm

On the left is an old tree close to the Convent (I think an olive) to which Wellington's horse was tied while waiting for him.

Full sure should fall a prey. He in his pride
Scorned the poor numbers of the English foe,
And thought the children of the land would fly
From his advance, like sheep before the wolf,
Scattering, and lost in terror. Ill he knew
The Lusitanian spirit! Ill he knew
The arm, the heart, of England! Ill he knew
Her Wellington! He learnt to know them here,
That spirit and that arm, that heart, that mind,
Here on Busaco gloriously displayed,
When, hence repulsed, the beaten boaster wound
Below his course circuitous, and left
His thousands for the beasts and ravenous fowl.
The Carmelite who in his cell recluse
Was wont to sit, and from a skull receive
Death's silent lesson, wheresoe'er he walk,
Henceforth may find his teachers. He shall find
The Frenchmen's bones in glen and grove, on rock
And height, where'er the wolves and carrion birds
Have strewn them, washed in torrents, bare and bleached
By sun and rain, and by the winds of heaven.

Robert Southey.

Note (to Fr. José da S. Silvestre's *Diary*) regarding the seventy French wounded abandoned by Masséna near Moura.

In Beamish's *History of the Kings German Legion*, there occurs the following passage:

Early on the morning of the 29th large bodies of men were discernible from the heights, and General Craufurd, not being able to ascertain at that distance of what description of persons they were composed, sent down Captain von Linsengen with his squadron to ascertain the point. After scrambling with difficulty over the numerous dead bodies, by which their path was blocked up, the hussars reached the crowd, and found it to consist of Portuguese peasants, who were assembled round from 300 to 400 wounded men, who had been abandoned by the enemy. These unfortunate creatures had been so disabled that they were unable to move, and they now lay in momentary expectation of being murdered by the peasants.
On seeing the hussars they implored their protection, which

was readily given; some litters that were found in the field afforded means of transport, and driving off the peasants, the Germans succeeded in getting the unfortunate fellows conveyed to the neighbouring convent, where they were taken in charge by the monks.

Fr. Jose states the number of these wounded at seventy, and he is more likely to be right than Von Linsengen, because the men were under his care for a long time. The only mistake made by Fr. Jose is with regard to the means used in bringing the men to the chapel. He thought they were brought on the troopers' horses, but it is more probable that, according to Von Linsengen's statement, they were brought on the litters found in the field. In some cases, possibly, horses might have been used to carry some of those who had not legs broken. It will be noticed that out of seventy brought by the Germans and twelve by the monks, only twelve died—the rest having been ordered by Col. Trant to the Hospital at Oporto.

Prof. Oman mentions Von Linsengen's account of the finding of these four hundred men, and their being taken to the convent, but he goes on to say:

> What became of them afterwards it is well not to speculate. No friendly column came that way again (unless some of Reynier's rear-guard cavalry may have looked in at Bussaco on the 30th, when Craufurd had gone. This is possible. Trant's Portuguese were back in the place on Oct. 4) and the Ordenanza were daily growing more exasperated at the conduct of the invading army.

Through the humanity of our good monk all these men were saved from the peasants, and the French might well erect a monument to his memory at the chapel, though perhaps many people will think his kindly memory will be kept warm in all hearts through the medium of his *Diary*, and that no other monument is required.

It may be noted that Prof. Oman guesses that some of Reynier's rear-guard cavalry might have looked in at Bussaco on the 30th September.

No cavalry came back to Bussaco from the Mortagoa side. The two pickets that came belonged to Ney's Corps, and they came from the opposite direction, *i.e.* from the main body marching to Coimbra, below Botao.

Prof. Oman is also in error in saying that Trant's Portuguese were back in the place on October 4th. A picket came as far as Moura on October 5th, and a sergeant and a few men came as far as the chapel to see the wounded, and then returned to Mortagoa.

They probably belonged to Wilson's command.

As regards the English "general" said to have been mortally wounded on the 26th September, I think this must have been Captain Hoey, Deputy Assistant Adjutant-General.

Appendix

Extract from diary of a cavalry officer by the late Lieut. Col. William Tomkinson, 16th Light Dragoons. (Republished by Leonaur as *With Wellington's Cavalry*)

Sept. 26th.—At 2 p.m. we returned to the ground we had before occupied at the foot of Bosoac. The whole army was in position along the Sierra, and General Hill moved across this day from his ground at the Ponte Murcella. The enemy have closed up their whole force to the hills in front of the position, and a general action is expected. From the nature of our position, I cannot think the enemy will make any serious attack. The descent in places is so steep and great that a person alone cannot, without holding and choosing his ground, get down. I cannot think they will be so imprudent as to make it a general affair. We have 52,000 men, and their superiority is by no means equal to the advantage we have from position. They may calculate that the Portuguese troops, of which the greater part of the army is composed, will run away. I think we have rather above 20,000 English, the remainder Portuguese. The army ran from right to left as follows:

2nd Division:	Lieutenant-General Hill.
5th "	Major-General Leith's Corps.
3rd "	Major-General Picton.
1st "	Lieutenant-General Sir Brent Spencer.
Light "	Brigadier-General Crawford.
4th "	Major-General Cole.

General Anson found one squadron for duty with the Light Division, and the Heavy Brigade one in rear of the 1st Division. All were ordered to stand to their arms before daylight, the troops bivouacked as they stood in position, with their generals at the heads of divisions and brigades. Lord Wellington remained in the wood near the convent

MAJOR-GENERAL COLE

in the centre of the line. Everyone expected and wished a general attack at daylight. The army is in most beautiful order, and the Portuguese as fine-looking men and as steady under arms as any in the world. The only doubt rests with them; if they do their duty, and the business becomes general, there can be no doubt of success.

The 16th, at night, retired a short way for forage, no baggage allowed on the hill, but sent to the rear near Mealhada.

Sept. 27th.—The troops at daylight were all under arms, anxiously waiting the enemy's attack. All was quiet for some time, and as there was nothing to delay the enemy that we were aware of, Lord W. ordered patrols to our left, from General Anson's brigade. I was sent on one, and about 9 a.m. got on the hills lineable with our position. I there saw the attack on the Light Division; and on ascertaining that no troops had moved to the left, I returned to the regiment, which I found in the old ground where I had left it.

Note on the road of communication made by order of Wellington behind the crest of the Serra from end to end of the Allied position.

This road can still be traced. It was made principally by the villagers and the Portuguese troops.

Prof. Oman calls it a rough country road, and appears unaware of the fact that great labour was expended on it under the directions of Wellington's engineers. To connect the two parts of it extending to the right and left of the convent woods, the walls of that enclosure were broken through, so that the artillery and troops could easily pass from one part of the defence to another, and enabling a retreat to be safely conducted if necessary. On the night of the 28th September most of the artillery retired by this route, and Craufurd with the Light Division was left in the enclosure, with orders to defend the position to the last man.

The road of communication connected together the five routes to the low country, *viz. via* Villa Nova, *via* Bussaco and Luso, the road *via* the S. Antonio do Cantaro Pass, the road from Gondolem, and the track passing the Serra at the extreme right. Wyld's Map gives the trace of the whole road of communication between these points of crossing, but omits to show the point of passage through the convent enclosure walls.

THE ROADS ON THE ALLIED LEFT.

Extract from a report by Lieut. Bell, Assistant Quartermaster-General of the Light Division, upon the road from Mortagoa to Villa Nova and Meal-

hada, dated 22nd September, 1810.

This road is completely concealed, except in passing the small ridge between Mora and Mortagoa. From the crossing near Parada to Villa Nova, it follows the course of a small stream in a deep ravine, which cuts the Sierra de Busaco at its northern extremity, about two miles and a half from the wall of the convent park. Villa Nova is in the open country in rear of the Sierra, and only one league from Mealhada.

The road is an excellent car road, but perhaps hardly wide enough in some places for British artillery. At present, and during all the dry season, it affords an easier and quicker line of march for troops than the road by the convent, as it is neither so steep nor so winding as the other.

N.B.—The above explains why Wellington extended his left so far. It was necessary to cover the road named.

Extract from a letter from the Quartermaster-General to Sir Stapleton Cotton, dated Convent of Bussaco, 24th September, 1810.

Lord Wellington wishes you to send a patrol along the road that leads from Mortagoa to Sardao. That road, on leaving Mortagoa, passes through Gandra, Maceira, Orestal, and Boialva, to Sardao. The object is to obtain a report upon that road, and ascertain whether it is perfectly practicable or not for artillery. An officer should, therefore, be sent along with the patrol who is qualified to judge of the road in that respect. The patrol had better enter upon the road somewhere near Boialva, and proceed from thence towards Mortagoa, for it is desirable to avoid shewing the patrol to the enemy, or attracting his attention towards the road in question.

N.B.—This is the road afterwards discovered by the French cavalry under the guidance of a Spaniard, or Portuguese, whom they captured. It was used to turn the Allied left.

G. Murray, Q.M.G., to Lieut.-Gen. Hill.

Convent of Busaco, 25th Sept., 1810.

When upon the Sierra, the troops are to be kept a little behind the ridge, so that they may not be seen by the enemy until it becomes necessary to move them up on the ridge to repel an attack. You are to leave Major-General Fane with the cavalry under his orders in front of Ponte Murcella, and you will direct

Colonel Le Cor to place his division and guns upon the Sierra of Murcella.

Nothing will persuade me that Lord Wellington will risk losing his reputation. (But if he does) I hold him; tomorrow we will finish the conquest of Portugal, and in a few days I will drown the leopard.

Masséna, to Generals Eble and Fririon, who suggested on the 26th Sept. that the Allied position should be turned.

You are of the Army of the Rhine, you all love manoeuvring: this is the first time that Wellington appears disposed to give battle, and I wish to profit by the occasion.

Wellington to the Earl of Liverpool.

Coimbra, 30th Sept., 1810.

To the Earl of Liverpool.

While the enemy was advancing from Celorico and Trancoso upon Viseu, the different divisions of militia and Ordenanza were employed upon their flanks and rear; and Col. Trant with his division attacked the escort of the military chest and reserve artillery near Tojal, on the 20th inst. He took two officers and eighty prisoners, but the enemy collected a force from the front and rear, which obliged him to retire again towards the Douro. I understand that the enemy's communication is completely cut off, and he possesses only the ground upon which his army stands.

My dispatch of the 20th inst. will have informed you of the measures which I had adopted and which were in progress to collect the army in this neighbourhood, and, if possible, to prevent the enemy from obtaining possession of this town.

On the 21st the enemy's advanced guard pushed on to Sta Combadao, at the junction of the rivers Criz and Dad; and Brig.-Gen. Pack retired across the former and joined Brig.-Gen. Craufurd at Mortagoa, having destroyed the bridges over those two rivers. The enemy's advance guard crossed the Criz, having repaired the bridge, on the 23rd, and the whole of the 6th Corps was collected on the other side of the river. I therefore withdrew the cavalry through the Serra de Busaco, with the exception of three squadrons, as the ground was unfavourable for the operation of that arm.

On the 25th the whole of the 6th and of the 2nd Corps crossed the Criz in the neighbourhood of Sta Combadao; and Brig.-Gen. Pack's brigade and Brig.-Gen. Craufurd's division retired to the position which I had fixed upon for the army on the top of the Serra de Busaco. These troops were followed in this movement by the whole of the corps of Ney and Regnier (the 6th and the 2nd); but it was conducted by Brig.-Gen. Craufurd with great regularity, and the troops took their position without sustaining any loss of importance. The 4th Portuguese Caçadores, which had retired on the right of the other troops, and the piquets of the 3rd Division of infantry, which were posted at S. Antonio do Cantaro, under Major Smyth of the 45th Regiment, were engaged with the advance of Regnier's corps in the afternoon, and the former showed that steadiness and gallantry which others of the Portuguese troops have since manifested.

The Serra de Busaco is a high ridge which extends from the Mondego in a northerly direction about eight miles. At the highest point of the ridge, about two miles from its termination, is the convent and garden of Busaco. The Serra de Busaco is connected by a mountainous tract of country with the Serra de Caramula, which extends in a north-easterly direction beyond Viseu, and separates the valley of the Mondego from the valley of the Douro. On the left of the Mondego, nearly in a line with the Serra de Busaco, is another ridge of the same description, called the Serra da Murcella, covered by the River Alva, and connected by other mountainous parts with the Serra d'Estrella. All the roads to Coimbra from the eastward lead over the one or the other of these Serras. They are very difficult for the passage of an army, the approach to the top of the ridge on both sides being mountainous.

As the enemy's whole army was on the right of the Mondego, and it was evident that he intended to force our position, Lt.-Gen. Hill crossed that river by a short movement to his left, on the morning of the 26th, leaving Col. Le Cor with his brigade on the Serra da Murcella, to cover the right of the army, and Brig.-Gen. Fane, with his division of Portuguese cavalry and the 13th Light Dragoons in front of the Alva, to observe and check the movements of the enemy's cavalry on the Mondego.

With this exception, the whole army was collected upon the Serra de Busaco, with the British cavalry observing the plain in the rear of its left, and the road leading from Mortagoa to Oporto, through the mountainous tract which connects the Serra de Busaco with the Serra de Caramula.

The 8th Corps joined the enemy in our front on the 26th, but he did not make any serious attack on that day. The light troops on both sides were engaged throughout the line.

At six in the morning of the 27th the enemy made two desperate attacks upon our position, the one on the right, the other on the left of the highest part of Serra. The attack upon the right was made by two divisions of the 2nd Corps, on that part of the Serra occupied by the 3rd Division of infantry. One division of French infantry arrived at the top of the ridge, where it was attacked in the most gallant manner by the 88th Regiment under the command of Lt.-Col. Wallace, the 45th, under the command of Lt.-Col. the Hon. R. Meade, and by the 8th Portuguese Regiment, under the command of Lt.-Col. Douglas, directed by Major-Gen. Picton

These three corps advanced with the bayonet, and drove the enemy's division from the advantageous ground which they had obtained. The other division of the 2nd Corps attacked farther on the right, by the road leading by S. Antonio do Cantaro, also in front of Major-Gen. Picton's division. These were repulsed before they could reach the top of the ridge, by the 74th, under the command of Lt.-Col. the Hon. R. Trench, and the brigade of Portuguese Infantry of the 9th and 21st Regiments, under the command of Col. Champelmond, directed by Col. Mackinnon.

Major-Gen. Leith also moved to his left to the support of Major-Gen. Picton, and aided in the defeat of the enemy by the 3rd Battalion of Royals, the 1st Battalion of the 9th, and the 2nd Battalion of the 38th Regiments. In these attacks Major-Gens. Leith and Picton, Cols. Mackinnon and Champelmond, of the Portuguese service, who was wounded, Lt.-Col. Wallace, Lt.-Col. the Hon. R. Meade, Lt.-Col. Sutton, of the 9th Portuguese, Major Smyth of the 45th, who was afterwards killed, Lt.-Col. Douglas, and Major Birmingham, of the 8th Portuguese Regiments, distinguished themselves.

Major-Gen. Picton reports the good conduct of the 9th and

21st Portuguese Regiments, commanded by Col. Sutton and Lt.-Col. A. Bacellar, and of the Portuguese artillery, under the command of Major Arenschildt. I have also to mention, in a particular manner, the conduct of Captain Dansey of the 88th. Major-Gen. Leith reports the good conduct of the Royals, 1st Battalion and 9th, and 2nd Battalion of the 38th Regiments; and I beg to assure your Lordship that I have never witnessed a more gallant attack than that made by the 88th, 45th, and 8th Portuguese Regiments, on the enemy's division which had reached the ridge of the Serra.

On the left, the enemy attacked with three divisions of infantry of the 6th Corps, on the part of the Serra occupied by the Light Division of infantry, commanded by Brig.-Gen. Craufurd and by the brigade of Portuguese infantry, commanded by Brig.-Gen. Pack. One division of infantry only made any progress to the top of the hill, and they were immediately charged with the bayonet by Brig.-Gen. Craufurd, with the 43rd, 52nd, and 95th, and the 3rd Portuguese Caçadores, and driven down with immense loss. Brig.-Gen. Coleman's brigade of Portuguese infantry, which was in reserve, was moved up to the right of Brig.-Gen. Craufurd's division, and a battalion of the 19th Portuguese Regiment, under the command of Lt.-Col. MacBean, made a gallant and successful charge upon a body of another division of the enemy, which was endeavouring to penetrate in that quarter. In this attack, Brig.-Gen Craufurd, Lt.-Cols. Beckwith, of the 95th, and Barclay, of the 52nd, and the commanding officers of the regiments, distinguished themselves.

Besides these attacks, the light troops of the two armies were engaged throughout the 27th; and the 4th Portuguese Caçadores and the 1st and 15th Regiments, directed by Brig.-Gen. Pack, and commanded by Lt.-Col. Hill, Lt.-Col. Luis do Rego, and Major Armstrong, showed great steadiness and gallantry.

The loss sustained by the enemy in his attack of the 27th has been numerous. I understand that the Generals of Division, Merle, Loison, and Maucune are wounded, and Gen. Simon was taken prisoner by the 52nd Regiment, and three colonels—officers, and 250 men. The enemy left 2,000 killed upon the field of battle, and I understand from the prisoners and deserters that the loss in wounded is immense.

The enemy did not renew his attack, excepting by the fire of his light troops on the 28th; but he moved a large body of infantry and cavalry from the left of his centre to the rear, from whence I saw his cavalry his march on the road from Mortagoa over the mountains towards Oporto.

Having thought it probable that he would endeavour to turn our left by that road, I had directed Col. Trant, with his division of militia, to march to Sardao, with the intention that he should occupy the mountains, but unfortunately he was sent round by Oporto, by the general officer commanding in the north, in consequence of a small detachment of the enemy being in possession of S. Pedro do Sul; and, notwithstanding the efforts which he made to arrive in time, he did not reach Sardao till the 28th, at night, after the enemy were in possession of the ground.

As it was probable that, in the course of the night of the 28th, the enemy would throw the whole of his army upon the road, by which he could avoid the Serra de Busaco and reach Coimbra by the high road of Oporto, and thus the army would have been exposed to be cut off from that town, or to a general action in less favourable ground, and as I had reinforcements in my rear, I was induced to withdraw from the Serra de Busaco.

The enemy did break up in the mountains at 11 at night of the 28th, and he made the march I expected. His advanced guard was at Avelans, on the road from Oporto to Coimbra, yesterday, and the whole army was seen in march through the mountains. That under my command, however, was already in the low country, between the Serra de Busaco and the sea, and the whole of it, with the exception of the advanced guard, is this day on the left of the Mondego.

Although, from the unfortunate circumstances of the delay of Col. Trant's arrival at Sardao, I am apprehensive that I shall not succeed in effecting the object I had in view in passing the Mondego and in occupying the Serra de Busaco, I do not repent my having done so. This movement has afforded me a favourable opportunity of showing the enemy the description of troops of which this army is composed; it has brought the Portuguese levies into action with the enemy for the first time in an advantageous situation; and they have proved that the trouble which has been taken with them has not been thrown away, and that they are worthy of contending in the same ranks with British troops in this interesting cause, which they afford the best hopes of saving.

Throughout the contest on the Serra, and in all the previous marches, and those which we have since made, the whole army have conducted themselves in the most regular manner. Accordingly, all the operations have been carried on with ease; the soldiers have suffered no privations, have undergone no unnecessary fatigue, there has been no loss of stores, and the army is in the highest spirits.

I have received throughout the service the greatest assistance from the general and staff officers. Lt.-Gen. Sir B. Spencer has given the assistance his experience enables him to afford me; and I am particularly indebted to the adjutant and the quarter-master-generals, and the officers of their departments, and to Lt.-Col. Bathurst, and the officers of my personal staff; to Major-Gen. Howorth and the artillery, and particularly to Lt.-Col. Fletcher, Capt. Chapman, and the officers of the Royal Engineers. I must likewise mention Mr. Kennedy and the officers of the commissariat, which department has been carried on most successfully.

I should not do justice to the service, or to my own feelings, if I did not take this opportunity of drawing your Lordship's attention to the merits of Marshal Beresford. To him exclusively, under the Portuguese Government, is due the merit of having raised, formed, disciplined, and equipped the Portuguese Army, which has now shown itself capable of engaging and defeating the enemy. I have besides received from him all the assistance which his experience and abilities and his knowledge of this country have qualified him to afford me.

The enemy have made no movement in Estremadura, or in the northern provinces, since I addressed your Lordship last.

My last accounts from Cadiz are of the 9th instant.

I enclose a return of the killed and wounded of the Allied armies in the course of the 25th, 26th, and 27th.

I send this dispatch by my *aide-de-camp*, Capt. Burgh, to whom I beg to refer your Lordship for any further details, and I recommend him to your Lordship's notice.

To the Rt. Hon. W. W. Pole.

Leiria, 4th Oct., 1810

My dear William,

The croakers about useless battles will attack me again on that of Bussaco, notwithstanding that our loss was really trifling: but I should have been inexcusable if, knowing what I did, I had not endeavoured to stop the enemy then, and I should have stopped him entirely if it had not been for the blunders of the Portuguese General commanding in the North, who was prevented by a small French patrol from sending Trant up the road by which he was ordered to march. If he came by that road, the French could not have turned our position and they must have attacked us again: they could not have carried it and they must have retired.

The question is whether, having it in my power to take such a position, it was right to incur the risk of a general engagement in it. That which has since happened shows that, if not turned, I could have maintained it without loss of importance, and that if turned I could retire from it without inconvenience: and under these circumstances there could be no doubt. To this add that the battle has had the best effects in inspiring confidence in the Portuguese troops, both among our croaking officers and the people of the country.

This likewise removed an inference which began to be very general, that we intended to fight no more, but to retire to our ships: and it has given the Portuguese troops a taste for an amusement to which they were not before accustomed, and which they would not have acquired if I had not put them in a very strong position.

Whether the Battle of Bussaco is approved or not, I believe anybody will admit that the movements by which the British Army was collected in and afterwards removed from that position were very satisfactory. Indeed, the French themselves are astonished at our having been able to bring Hill up to that point in so short a time.

Wellington.

Ney's Attack at Bussaco.

Masséna's orders were (26th Sept., 1810):

The 6th Corps will attack by the two roads which lead upon the route of Coimbra. One of its divisions will form its reserve, and its Artillery will be placed in different positions to be able to sustain it as required. M. the Marshal Ney will dispose his two columns of attack in such a way as to deliver his attack when Gen. Regnier shall be master of the heights and when he (Regnier) shall march upon the Convent of Bussaco. It will be for Marshal Ney to press his attack if he sees that the enemy advances to make a movement upon Gen. Regnier, or if the enemy makes a movement of retreat.

Marshal Ney is too much dependent upon the suitable time for his movement for it to be determined for him.

He will be preceded by his skirmishers. Once arrived upon the crest he will form line of battle for the combined final movements of the army.

The 8th Corps will assemble behind the village of Mora at 6 a.m., etc. etc. Its artillery will be placed so as to stop the enemy if he makes a forward movement.

The following is the report made to the quartermaster-general by Major Sturgeon of the Royal Staff Corps, in compliance with instructions.

Position of the British and Portuguese troops in the vicinity of the Convent of Bussaco on the 26th September, 1810:

The Brigade of Guards. Towards the right extremity of table-land, where the beacon is situated at the top of the Serra.

4th Dragoon Guards. In reserve behind the Foot Guards.

Cameron's Brigade. On the left of the Guards.

Pakenham's Brigade. On the left of Cameron's.

Pack's Portuguese Brigade Between Pakenham's Brigade and the park wall of the convent.

One 9-pounder and one Howitzer. On a platform formed by a rocky projection in front of Pack's Brigade.

Four 9-pounders. On an advantageous position near the right of the infantry.

A brigade of 3-pounders, Portuguese mountain guns Intermediate between the expounders.

A brigade of Hanoverian 6-pounders. In front of the eastern gate of the park of the convent.

The Light Division. On a projecting part of the position, overlooking the villages Mora and Sul.

The troop of Horse Artillery attached to the Light Division One half commanding Mora and its vicinity. The other half commanding the slopes in the neighbourhood of Sul.

A Brigade of Portuguese 3-pounders Intermediate between the artillery on the right of the Light Division, and the German artillery in front of the park gate.

The infantry of the King's German Legion. On the high ground in front of the Chapel of Almas de Incarnador, in second line to the Light Division.

Two brigades of Portuguese infantry. In column, as a reserve, between the park wall and the Chapel of Almas de Incarnador.

Position of the French Troops on the 26th of Sept, 1810.

That part of the French Army, which had moved forward by the great road leading from Mortagoa to Bussaco, through the village of Mora, was irregularly placed on each side of the road along the line of their march.

Towards the evening of the 26th, bodies of infantry, from different points along the main road, filed down the different slopes leading into the ravine, on our left of the village of Sul, and were assembled in the pine groves on the right side of the ravine; and another strong column was formed by the enemy on the reverse of a hill immediately behind the chapel of Mora, and to our right of that village. These dispositions seemed to threaten a combined attack upon the Light Division.

The French cavalry, which had continued throughout the day on a retired position upon our right of the road to Mortagoa, began, towards sunset, to file to their left towards the village of Cerdeira. But this appeared to be merely a movement of convenience.

The left column of the French Army was upon high ground near the road which leads from Mortagoa to the pass over the Serra of Bussaco, by the village of S. Antonio do Cantaro.

Events of the 27th of September.

About six o'clock in the morning.—The engagement was begun by the artillery, and by the sharpshooters, on both sides. The smoke prevented my counting the number of guns brought forward by the enemy, to favour their attack on that part of the position occupied by the Light Division; but the superiority of the fire seemed to be from our side.

About forty minutes past six.—The enemy formed a column of infantry near Mora, which marched irregularly but quickly into that village; and, about seven o'clock, an attack was made upon the Light Division. The enemy's troops arrived at the crest of the heights behind which the 43rd and 52nd infantry, etc., were all drawn up, but they were almost instantaneously repelled, driven down the slopes, and pursued beyond the village of Sul. During the advance of the enemy to make the attack, a Portuguese regiment had been moved to support the left of the Light Division; and when that division moved forward its place was immediately occupied by the King's German Legion; but these troops resumed each their respective original positions when the Light Division returned from pursuing the enemy.

Coleman's Portuguese Brigade had also moved forward, in column, towards that part of the position, on the right of the Light Division, where the Portuguese 3-pounders were; and it afterwards formed in line, in front of the eastern park-wall of the convent, where the abattis in front of the gate, as well as the wall on each side of it, was lined with musketry.

After this, sharpshooters were warmly engaged on both sides, particularly from our left of the village of Sul to our right of the village of Cerquedo. About nine o'clock the enemy pushed forward his sharp-shooters, in very considerable numbers, to a rocky eminence in front of the right regiment of Coleman's Brigade; but that regiment repulsed them, and the whole of the brigade made a forward movement till recalled by Lord Wellington.

★★★★★★

This rocky eminence has now been partly quarried away, but the remains of it can be seen in the large photograph of the "funnel ravine," below the "Monumento" and a little to its left. It is possible that the "right regiment" was commanded by Major MacBean, that it drove the French from the *rocky eminence*, and defeated them on the road below. Sir William MacBean says the French retired before his battalion to the road below, but he continued his advance, driving the enemy from the road to the bottom of the ravine. His account fits in with Major Sturgeon's observations; but the two accounts differ in respect to the formation of the French. I have discussed this matter elsewhere.

★★★★★★

The *caçadores* of General Pack's Portuguese Brigade made also a forward movement down the slope, but were recalled by General Pack.

This advance, in force, of the enemy's sharpshooters appeared to be intended as a prelude to an attack by a strong column of infantry, which had been forming, at the same time, on our right of the village of Mora.

But that column being disturbed by the fire of the 9-pounders on the tableland of the Serra, retired to the reverse of the hill behind, where it remained formed in column. Having been directed, after this, by the quartermaster-general to proceed with the sketch of the position I had been engaged in, I ceased to have an opportunity to observe, in a connected manner, the further operations which took place.

Henry Sturgeon, Major,
Royal Staff Corps.

Notes on Major Sturgeon's Report.

In Wyld's Memoir of his Maps will be found the foregoing report to the quartermaster-general, by Major Sturgeon, of the Royal Staff Corps, who was directed to take notes of what he observed in the battle and to take the time of each occurrence. The important points noticeable are:

(1) That Cameron's Brigade was on the left of Stopford's and that Pakenham's was to the left of Cameron.

(2) That Pack's Portuguese Brigade was between Pakenham's Brigade and the park wall of the convent.

(3) One 9-pounder and one Howitzer, on a platform formed by a rocky projection in front of Pack's Brigade.

(4) Four 9-pounders in an advantageous position near the right of the infantry (*i.e.* I presume near Stopford's right).

(5) A brigade of 3-pounder Portuguese mountain guns, intermediate between the 9-pounders (which is vague).

(6) A brigade of Hanoverian 6-pounders in front of the Eastern gate (Porta da Sulla) of the park of the convent. I take these to be Cleeve's.

(7) Troop of Horse Artillery attached to Light Division, *i.e.* Ross's: three guns commanding Moira and its vicinity; three guns commanding the slopes in the neighbourhood of Sul.

(8) Brigade of Portuguese 3-pounders intermediate between

the artillery on the right of the Light Division and the German artillery in front of the park gate.

As regards (1): It may be remarked that Prof. Oman places Pakenham in the middle of the 1st Division, and Blantyre, or Cameron, on the left, whereas Major Sturgeon says Pakenham was on the left and Blantyre, *i.e.* Cameron, in the centre of that Division.

As regards (2): If Pack's Brigade was literally between Pakenham and the park wall this would naturally be taken to mean that Pack was in line with the 1st Division. I think, however, it is meant that he was below the crest on the broken ground there, and in the quarries.

As regards (3): There are several such rocky platforms in front of where Pack was, but the mention of the 9-pounder and the Howitzer is interesting; no other writer mentions this little battery as far as I know, and as four 9-pounders are immediately afterwards recorded, I think this must have been a brigade of five 9-pounders and one Howitzer, broken up as mentioned. The guns must have been Capt. Lawson's.

As regards (5): This brigade of 3-pounder mountain guns was almost certainly one of those two recently commanded by Major von Arentschildt.

As regards (6): Fr. Jose de S. Silvestre in his *Diary* states that near the Porta Sulla, inside, a battery was constructed to attack the enemy if he entered by this gate. Major Sturgeon says that a brigade of Hanoverian 6-pounders was placed in front of the above gate.

I take it that Cleeve's Battery of 6-pounders was placed outside that it could be quickly taken in by the gate and placed in the battery constructed there.

Gen. Coleman's Portuguese Division was on the left of this gate and Major MacBean commanded a regiment of it. It is singular that he states, twenty-three years afterwards, that the only Germans he saw were of Major Hartmann's Brigade of Artillery. The batteries commanded by this officer were Rettberg's and Thompson's, both of which were on the high plateau and to the right of it, where Major MacBean did not go, so that he was mistaken in his recollections. It must have been Capt. Cleeve's German Battery which he saw.

As regards (7): Ross's guns were placed with three guns commanding Sula and three, Moira—but these villages were much in the same line—and the whole battery could be fired in either direction.

As regards (8): The guns at the head of the "funnel ravine" were apparently located as follows: Cleeve's and Passos's 6-pounders near the

Porta da Sulla; Mountain Battery 3-pounders near the site of "Monumento."

The effects of Capt. Ross's guns, which had pounded this column in its advance, were fearfully shown in the village of Bussaco (i.e. Sula). Fragments of cottages, shreds of clothing, and bodies and limbs shattered, met the sight of the pursuers as they again returned to the ridge.

When the head of Simon's column appeared in the act of deploying and the 52nd advanced to charge, Capt. William Jones, more commonly known in the division as Jack Jones, a fiery Welshman, rushed upon the *chef de bataillon*, who was in the act of giving the word to his men, and killed him on the spot with a blow of his sword. Jones immediately cut off the medal with which the major was decorated and affixed it to himself. Simon surrendered to Private James Hopkins, of Robert Campbell's company, who received a pension of twenty pounds *per annum* as a reward for his bravery on this occasion. Private Harris, of 52nd, also shared in his capture and got a pension.

History of Rifle Brigade

25th Sept., 1810.—The right wing of the battalion under Beckwith was halted in the valley of Sula, where they were smartly cannonaded from the opposite heights, but without loss; and at night they were withdrawn from Sula, leaving a picket in that village, and stationed among the rocks on the face of the hill, *right and left of the road leading to* Coimbra.

26th.—Skirmishing went on.

27th.—Among the rocks and broken ground on the sides of this hill were disposed the riflemen of this battalion (95th). Scarcely had day dawned when the enemy made his advance. Loison's division *climbed the road leading up the face of the projecting hill,* though galled by the fire of the riflemen and Ross's guns. Yet they came on, the riflemen, as the French pressed up the hill, running in on their supports and forming in the hollow between the spur and the mountain. At last the leading section topped the hill, and then, and not till then, Craufurd gave the signal. The bugles sounded, and 1,800 men sprang as from the earth. Instantaneously they gave a volley, the head of the column after one destructive fire from the leading section reeled. Craufurd ordered a charge, and soldiers, arms, and knapsacks and caps rolled down the hill.

The French column was wedged in the road. The leading sections were driven back on the still advancing rear, and all turned back in utter confusion. Thus, they came under the fire of the whole division, which far overlapped their flanks, and through the narrow street of Sula they fled, trampling the living and the dead.

In the afternoon Craufurd received a flag of truce with Gen. Simon's luggage, and granted a temporary cessation of arms.

40th Regiment.

Sergeant Lawrence relates:

I remember one very curious thing which occurred at this time (1810), which was that the names of the drum-majors of the three regiments collected in this place were—Sun, 53rd, Moon, 40th, Star, 9th Regiments. (40th with Gen. Cole.)

5th Battalion 60th Rifles' History.

From Major Woodgate to Lt.-Col. Davy

Alcointre, Dec. 24th, 1810.

My dear Davy,

Since my last to you we have had much to do, although by the papers and the mangled accounts of the affair of Bussaco you might fairly conclude we had nothing to do in that business.

The omission of our regiment (60th), among the number of those which distinguished themselves was owing to Gen. Picton not making a written report of the conduct of the division. The fact is, Lord W. was present during the whole affair, and on its termination thanked Gen. P., and said, "You need not make any report to me, I have seen the whole myself, and shall mention your division particularly."

You may suppose we were much astonished on the arrival of the despatch to find the efforts of the "Americans" had escaped his Lordship's notice. Col. Williams, who was in the thickest of the fight, and was twice wounded, was of course particularly annoyed, as he had a very fine command of light infantry who were engaged the whole day, and consisted of our three companies and those of the 45th, 88th, 74th, and 94th. (Meant 90th.) He applied to Gen. Picton, who, of course, expressed his sorrow for the omission, and wrote to him the letter which I shall transcribe on the other part of this paper.

I trouble you on this subject as I think you still feel an interest in some of those who are still in the battalion, and that this unusual omission of the 60th may be accounted for.

W. Woodgate.

Copy of Gen. Picton's letter to Col. Williams

Cordoceera, October 30th, 1810.

My dear Sir,

On reading over the Gazette account of the action of the 27th *ult.*, at Bussaco, I was most disappointed and concerned not to find your name among those of the C.O.'s of corps in the 3rd Division, who were particularly noticed on that occasion. You cannot have any doubt of my sentiments, as they were expressed in the Division Orders of that day. Yet I fear that I must take the blame to myself for the omission, having neglected to make a written report of the day to H.G.L.C. of Forces, who, being present on a commanding situation, and immediately contiguous to that part of the position defended by the 3rd Division, I conceived to be fully acquainted with the merits and services of each particular corps, but on reflection I find the post you defended (with the Light Corps of 2nd Division) with so much gallantry for so many hours was situated so low in the ravine of S. Antonio do Cantaro that he would not probably have seen your situation or witnessed your exertions, but you may be assured that I will take an early opportunity of mentioning to his Lordship that no commanding officer of any corps had more claim to public notice on that occasion than yourself.

Thos. Picton, Major-Gen.,
Comdg. 3rd Division.

To Lt.-Col. Williams,
Comdg. Light Corps, 3rd Division.

Note.—Picton formed a light corps for divisional purposes of the headquarters, and three companies of the 5th Battalion, 60th, and the light companies of the other regiments under him.

History of Connaught Rangers. Summary. Just before the charge.

The regiment was drawn up in line, many men had already fallen, the colours carried by Ensigns Joseph Owgan and William Grattan were pierced by numerous bullets, and three of the colour-sergeants were wounded.

Capt. Dunn returned and said that a body of riflemen had occupied a cluster of rocks on the right of the regiment, and the main body of the enemy was moving towards an open space which separated the 88th from 45th Regiment.

Lt.-Col. Wallace then threw the battalion into column, right in front, it had scarcely reached the rocks when a murderous fire, etc.

8th Portuguese Regiment not yet opened fire, it was too distant. (It was coming up from the right.—G.L.C.)

Four companies of 45th engaged in unequal combat. *Gwynne had already fallen* (not correct). 88th rushed to their assistance and two corps charged together.

One discharge and then the bayonet—French driven over the side.

Mentions three companies 88th at rocks, and refers to Capt. Dunn and Brazil.

Wellington said of Wallace and the 88th and 45th Regiments, "I never saw a more gallant charge."

Note.—Wellington included the 8th Portuguese.

Reminiscences of a Subaltern,
U.S. Magazine, 84, 4.

Lieut. Heppenstal of the 88th Regiment was near falling a sacrifice to the richness of his dress. He belonged to the light troops of the army at the Battle of Bussaco and was warmly engaged with the advance of the enemy. He was a man of the most determined bravery and gigantic strength, and more than once became personally engaged with the French riflemen.

At one time, carried away by his daring impetuosity, he pursued his successes so far as to be nearly mixed with the enemy: a number of Portuguese *caçadores* coming up at this moment mistook him for a French general officer and attempted to make him a prisoner. A scuffle ensued, in which he lost the skirts of his frockcoat, and it was not until an explanation took place that he was enabled to rejoin his regiment in this laughable trim, his beautiful gold-tagged frock being converted into a regular spencer.

Poor H. It was his first appearance under fire, and it was not difficult for those who witnessed his too gallant debut to foresee that his career of glory would be short. He carried a rifle, and his unerring aim brought down many a man on the morning I am speaking of, but he did not long survive the praises bestowed on him.

Adventures with Connaught Rangers, Grattan.
(Republished by Leonaur with both volumes in one edition.)
Edited by Prof. Oman.

This same Battle of Busaco was one of the most serious ever fought in the Peninsula, and, for this reason, it was the first in which the Portuguese lines were brought under fire, and upon their conduct in this—their maiden effort against their veteran opponent—depended the fate of Portugal, and the Peninsula also.

Such being the case, it must ever be classed as a very important event, and one that should be recorded by the historian with great care and fidelity; yet, strange to say, there is not, that I have read, any faithful report of it in print.

In vain do we turn even to Col. Napier's splendid history of the war in the Peninsula in expectation of finding a correct account, no such account is there to be found.

In all, therefore, that I am going to relate as to the part which the 3rd Division took in it, I shall keep as close as I can to what I know to be the facts.

On the morning of the 27th the haze was so thick that little could be seen at any great distance; but the fire of the light troops along the face of the hill put it beyond doubt that a battle would take place. Two guns belonging to Capt. Lane's troop of artillery were ordered upon the left of the 88th Regiment and immediately opened fire, while the Portuguese Battery, under the German Major Arentschildt, passed at a trot towards the Saint Antonio Pass in front of the 74th British.

A rolling fire of musketry and some discharges of cannon in the direction of S. Antonio announced what was taking place there; and the face of the hill immediately in front of the Brigade of Lightburne and to the left of the 88th Regiment was beginning to show that the efforts of the enemy were about to be directed against this portion of the ground held by the 3rd Division.

The fog cleared away and a bright sun enabled us to see what was passing before us. A vast crowd of *tirailleurs* was pressing forward with great ardour, and their fire as well as their numbers was so superior to that of our advance that some men of the brigade of Lightburne, as also a few of the 88th, were killed while standing in line. A colour-sergeant named Macnamara was shot through the head close beside myself and Ensign Owgan.

Col. King commanding the 5th Regiment, which was one of those belonging to Lightburne's Brigade, oppressed by the desultory fire he was unable to reply to without disturbing the formation of his battalion, brought his regiment a little out of its range, while Col. Alex. Wallace of the 88th took a file of men from each company of his regiment and, placing them under the command of Capt. George Bury and Lieut. William Mackie, ordered him to advance to the aid of our people, who were out-matched and roughly handled at the moment.

Our artillery still continued to discharge showers of grape and canister at half range, but the French light troops, fighting at open distance, heeded it not, and continued to multiply in great force. Nevertheless, in place of coming up direct in front of the 88th they edged off to their left out of sight of that corps, and far away from Lightburne's Brigade, and from the nature of the ground they would neither be seen nor their exact object defined. As they went to their left our advance inclined to the right, making a corresponding movement, but (though nothing certain could be known, as we soon lost sight of both parties) the roll of musketry never ceased and many of Bury's and Mackie's men returned wounded.

These two officers greatly distinguished themselves, and Bury, though badly injured, refused to quit the field. A soldier of Bury's company, of the name of Pollard, was shot through the shoulder, but seeing his captain, though wounded, continued at the head of his men, he threw off his knapsack and fought beside his officer; but this brave fellow's career of glory was short, a bullet penetrated the plate of his cap, passed through his brain, and he fell dead at B.'s feet. This was the sort of material the 88th were formed of, and these were the sort of men that were unnoticed by their general.

Lord W. was no longer to be seen, and Wallace and his regiment, standing alone without orders, had to act for themselves.

The colonel sent his captain of grenadiers (Dunne), to the right, where the rocks were highest (K) to ascertain how matters stood, for he did not wish at his own peril to quit the ground he had been ordered to occupy without some strong reason for so doing. All this time the brigade of Lightburne, as also the 88th, were standing at ordered arms.

In a few moments Dunne returned almost breathless; he said the rocks (A to B) were filling fast with Frenchmen, that a heavy column was coming up the hill *beyond the rocks*, and that the few companies of the 45th were about to be attacked.

Wallace asked if he thought half the 88th would be able to do the business.

'You will want every man,' was the reply.

Wallace, with a steady and cheerful countenance, turned to his men, and looking them full in the face said:

'Now, Connaught Rangers, mind what you are going to do, pay attention to what I have so often told you, and when I bring you face to face with these French rascals, drive them home to the muzzle. I have nothing more to say, and if I had, it would be no use, for in a minute or two there'll be such an infernal noise about your ears that you won't be able to hear yourselves.' This address went home to the hearts of us all, but there was no cheering. A steady but determined calm had taken the place of any lighter feeling, and it seemed as if the men had made up their minds to go to their work unruffled and not too much excited.

Wallace then threw the battalion from line into column *right in front* and moved on our side of the rocky point (K) at a quick pace. On reaching the rocks (A) he soon found it manifest that Dunne's report was not exaggerated—a number of Frenchmen were in possession of this cluster, and as soon as we approached within range, we were made to appreciate the effect of their fire—for our column was raked from front to rear.

The moment was critical, but Wallace, without being in the least taken aback, filed out the Grenadiers and the 1st Battalion Company commanded by Capts. Dunne and Dansey, and ordered them to storm the rocks, while he took the 5th Battalion Company, commanded by Capt. Oates, also out of the column, and ordered that officer to attack the rocks at the opposite side to that assailed by Dunne and Dansey.

This done, Wallace placed himself at the head of the remainder of the 88th and passed on to meet the French column.

At this moment the four companies of the 45th, commanded by Major Gwynne, a little on the *left* of the 88th and in front of that regiment, commenced their fire, but it in no way arrested the advance of the French column, as it with much order and regularity mounted the hill which, at this point, is rather flat. But here again another awkward circumstance occurred.

A battalion of the 8th Portuguese Infantry under Col. Douglas (?) posted on a rising ground on our right and a little in our rear, in place of advancing with us opened a distant and ill-directed fire, and one which would exactly cross the path of the

88th as that Corps was moving onward to meet the French column, which consisted of three splendid regiments—2nd Light Infantry, 36th and 70th of the line. (I doubt the 70th; he means 4th Leger.)

Wallace, seeing the loss and confusion that would infallibly ensue, sent Lieut. John Fitzpatrick, an officer of tried gallantry, with orders to point out to this regiment the error into which it had fallen, but F. had only time to take off his hat and call out 'Vamos Camarados' when he received two bullets, one from the Portuguese, which passed through his back, and the other in his left leg from the French, which broke the bone and caused a severe fracture, yet this regiment continued to fire away regardless of the consequences, and a battalion of militia, (Thomar Militia), which was immediately in rear of the 8th Portuguese took to their heels the moment the first volley was fired by their countrymen.

Wallace threw himself from his horse, and placing himself at the head of the 45th and 88th with Gwynne of the 45th on one side of him, and Capt. Seton of the 88th on the other, ran forward at a charging pace into the midst of the terrible flame in his front.

All was now confusion and uproar, smoke, fire, and bullets, officers, and soldiers, French drummers and French drums knocked down in every direction. British, French, and Portuguese mixed together, while in the midst of all was to be seen Wallace fighting like his ancestor of old at the head of his devoted followers, and calling out to his soldiers to 'press forward.'

Never was defeat more complete, and it was a proud moment for Wallace and Gwynne when they saw their gallant comrades breaking down and trampling under their feet this splendid division composed of some of the best troops the world could boast of.

The leading regiment, the 36th, one of Napoleon's favourite battalions, was nearly destroyed, upwards of 200 soldiers, and their old colonel covered with orders, lay dead in a small space, and the face of the hill was strewn with dead and wounded, which showed evident marks of the rapid execution done at this point, for Wallace never slackened his fire while a Frenchman was within his reach.

At daybreak French columns of attack advanced against the right of the English line with great impetuosity backed by a swarm of skirmishers, who quickly drove in the advanced pickets, and from their numerical superiority had nearly surrounded and cut off the picket of 79th when Capt. Neill Douglas gallantly volunteered with his company to go to its support, and opening fire from a favourable position checked the enemy's advance and enabled the picket to return in good order.

Unfortunately, Capt. Alexander Cameron was killed; he would not withdraw. Last seen by Capt. Douglas fighting hand to hand with several French soldiers, to whom he refused to deliver his sword. His body was found pierced with seven bayonet wounds.

Attack.—The attack (on the right) was soon abandoned.

79th was in Pakenham's Brigade on the high plateau.

U.S. Magazine, 1830, Part 2, 84, 4.
Recollections of a Subaltern.

At night we lay down to rest; each man with his firelock in his grasp remained at his post anxiously awaiting the arrival of the morrow, which was destined to be the last that many amongst us were to behold. We had no fires, and the deathlike stillness that reigned throughout our army was only interrupted by the occasional challenge of an advanced sentry, or a random shot fired at some imaginary foe. Some of us sat together chatting over the past, and guessing at the future; it was impossible not to regard the scene below us with feelings of awe.

An army of 65,000 or 70,000 warriors just returned from the conquest of Germany, covered with trophies, and commanded by officers inferior to none, lay within cannon shot of us, their demeanour too, argued a confidence in themselves which characterises the French soldier above any other in the world: more than 1,000 fires illuminated their camp, and we could perceive them in groups, either sitting round their blaze, or performing their ordinary avocations, with that sang-froid which alone belongs to men accustomed to danger. Our attitude though less brilliant was nevertheless an imposing one. We occupied an immense ridge studded with rocks, the very look of which was enough to impress an enemy with respect. Numerous batteries outtopped these natural defences: a line of 50,000 infantry, 25,000 of them British, were stationed at the summit of this terrific ridge, and the stern appearance of discipline which our bivouac presented must have impressed the enemy with an idea that its occupants were men of no ordinary stamp.

Circumstanced as I have described, the two armies lay, anxiously counting the hours which kept them asunder. The night at length passed away, and morning was ushered in by the warlike preparations of the enemy: on our side all was still as the grave. Lord W. lay amongst his soldiers under no other covering than his cloak, and the orders delivered by himself or his staff to prepare for the fight, were obeyed with cheerful promptitude.

In an instant the whole army was in battle array, Lord W. posted on an elevated spot immediately in rear of his 3rd Division. The enemy's attack was made at half-past six on the morning of the 27th September at two points, etc. etc. etc.

Our right was attacked if possible, with greater still impetuosity. Regnier headed this column and directed it to act against that part of the ridge occupied by the 3rd Division.

The 45th, 74th, and 88th British Regiments were formed in line a little in advance; the 8th Portuguese was on the right of these three battalions, while the 9th and 21st Portuguese occupied a post on the rear and the 5th and 83rd British were on the left of all.

The light troops of these corps vigorously attacked and drove back the enemy, but were in turn forced back themselves.

Col. Wallace of the 88th with promptitude reinforced his advance, by taking a few files from each battalion company, and thus aided, our men kept possession of the hill for a short time; but the overwhelming force which began to crowd upon them and which every moment multiplied, overpowered our riflemen, who were at length obliged to take refuge under the main body.

From the cloud of sharpshooters which crowned the heights immediately in front of the 88th Regiment Col. Wallace thought himself menaced by a dense body, and was in the act of telling his men the mode of attack he intended to adopt, when Capt. Dunne, who had been sent by the colonel to see what was going on on his right (for there was a heavy fog), returned with information that some hundred of the enemy's troops occupied a cluster of rocks close beside him, and that a column was moving over the open space between the 3rd and 5th Divisions, and as these rocks formed a pivot for their operations, the colonel formed the intention of changing his front, storming the rocks, and attacking the column.

At this time the 45th were engaged with numbers out of proportion, but they gallantly maintained their ground.

The 5th, 74th, and 83rd were likewise attacked, but the 88th from the nature of their situation came in contact with the full body of the enemy, and while opposed to three times their number in front were assailed on their left by a couple of hundred riflemen stationed on the rocks.

Col. Wallace changed his front, but had scarcely reached the rocks, when a fire, as destructive as it was animated, assailed him. The moment was a critical one, but he never lost his presence of mind. He ordered his two front companies to attack the rocks, while he pressed forward with the remainder of his regiment against the main body. The 8th Portuguese were close on the enemy and opened a well-directed fire, while the 45th were performing prodigies of valour. At this moment the 88th came up to the assistance of their comrades and the three regiments pressed on—a terrific contest took place. The French fought well, but they had no chance with our men when we grappled close with them; and they were overthrown, leaving half of their column on the heather, with which the hill was covered.

While the 88th, 45th, and 8th Portuguese were thus engaged the two companies of the 88th had a severe struggle with the riflemen in the rocks. The French, ranged amphitheatrically above the other, took a murderous aim at our soldiers in their advance to dislodge them, officers as well as privates became personally engaged in a hand-to-hand fight.

Capt. Dunne fought with his sabre—while Capt. Dansey made use of a firelock and bayonet; he received three wounds—and Capt. Dunne owed his life to a sergeant of his company named Brazill, who, seeing his officer in danger of being overpowered, scrambled to his assistance and making a thrust of his halbert at the Frenchman, transfixed him against the rock he was standing on. A contest of this sort could not possibly be of long duration, but it was nevertheless of a very serious kind. The enemy were numerous, well-disciplined, and full of ardour, and besides, from the nature of their position, they had but the alternative of driving our men down, or being themselves flung from the crags amongst which they fought.

The latter was the result—for although they combated with a desperation suited to the situation in which they were placed, the heroes of Austerlitz, Essling, and Wagram were hunted from the rocks by the Rangers of Connaught. (Picton always called the 88th by this name.)

Lord Wellington was a close observer of these attacks. He bestowed the warmest encomiums on the troops engaged, and Capt. Dansey had the rare good fortune to be noticed in his despatch detailing this battle.

One short hour made a great alteration in the appearance of the hill. The face of it, which a little before presented so animated a picture, was now as tranquil as before the commencement of the action, and were it not for the melancholy pledges which the dead and dying gave of the scene that had been passing, its reality might be doubted, so sudden was the enemy's attack and so complete its failure.

Our 5th Division under Gen. Leith inflicted a severe loss on the enemy in their flight down the hill, and their loss altogether was about 5,000.

The cluster of rocks presented a curious as well as melancholy side, one side of the base being strewed with our brave fellows, almost all of them shot through the head.

In many of the niches were to be seen dead Frenchmen in the posture they had fought, some sitting upright with their firelocks in their hands, others with their heads resting on the point of a rock, apparently in the act of taking a deliberate aim; while at the other side and on the projecting crags lay many who in an effort to escape the firing of our men were dashed to pieces in their fall.

The most part of what the writer of this sketch writes now came under his own immediate observation, but happening to be in the brigade of the 3rd Division, which so distinguished itself on that day, he cannot forbear paying his tribute of praise to the memory of Major Smith of the 45th, who fell at the head of that regiment, leading it on to one of those sanguinary attacks of which the writer has given a faint outline, nor to the intrepidity of Col. Alexander Wallace, who directed and executed the combined attack made by his corps.

Mounted on a grey charger, this officer led on the 88th to a most determined charge with the bayonet, but the noise of the enemy's bullets and the cheering of our soldiers so terrified the animal that he would not advance with the regiment; but the colonel dismounted and fought on foot at the head of his men amidst the hottest of the fire.

History of the 74th Highlanders.

The right brigade was thus distributed: the 74th across the road leading from S. Antonio do Cantaro to Coimbra, having two Portuguese guns on its right, and still further to the right the 9th and 21st Portuguese Regiments. On the left of the 74th was the 8th Portuguese, and beyond them the 88th and 45th Regiments, occupying the crest of a hill considerably to the left.

Shortly before daybreak on the 27th of September, the French formed five columns of attack, three of their 6th Corps, under Marshal Ney, against the left of the British position, occupied by the light division, and two of their 2nd Corps, under Gen. Regnier, against the third division.

The advance of these two last-mentioned columns was preceded by a cannonade from fourteen pieces of artillery, which caused some casualties in the ranks of the regiment. Capt. Langlands, of the 74th, had a narrow escape; he was knocked down by a 9-pounder shot, which passed through his cap, and was supposed to be killed, but he rose again uninjured, and was congratulated by Major-Gen. Picton on his good fortune. It being very tiring to the young soldiers, of whom the 74th Regiment was chiefly composed, to be kept standing inactive when now under fire for the first time, Col. Trench shortly addressed them, calling upon them to remember Assaye, and to imitate the former distinguished conduct of the regiment in India.

Both columns of the enemy advanced to the attack of the allied position, with the usual impetuous rush of French troops, and preceded by a cloud of skirmishers. Of these columns the one to the left was, on reaching the top of the ridge, occupied by the 88th and 45th Regiments, attacked and driven back by them after a severe and gallant contest. Meanwhile, the other column advanced upon the 74th, by the road from S. Antonio do Cantaro; the two right companies of the regiment were immediately detached, with the rifle companies belonging to the brigade, and drove back the enemy's skirmishers with great vigour, nearly to the foot of the Sierra.

★★★★★★

Lieut. Alves, who belonged to one of these companies, says in his journal: "The pleasure I experienced in advancing after the enemy, instead of remaining exposed and inactive as we were, cannot be expressed." This officer (now Major of the Depot Battalion in the Isle of Wight) was present with the 74th during every march and service in which it was engaged, from its first landing in the Peninsula until its return home in 1814, without one single day's absence from the regiment throughout the period. To the journal kept by him, in which the date of every event was noted at the time it occurred, the accuracy of the regimental record is chiefly attributable. Major Alves has received the war medal, and clasps, for eleven battles.

★★★★★★

The first advance of the French column was repulsed by the close and steady fire of the regiment, aided by the 9th and 21st Portuguese, before it reached the top of the ridge; but the attack was renewed with greater numbers to force the road guarded by the 74th; and the 8th Portuguese on its left, being thrown into confusion, the 74th Regiment was placed in a most critical situation, with its left flank exposed to the overwhelming force of the enemy. Fortunately, Gen. Leith had observed the danger, and detached two regiments (the 9th and 38th) of the 5th Division, which, passing from the right, along the rear of the 74th, in double-quick time, the leading regiment (the 9th) met the head of the French column, just as it crowned the ridge, in the space vacated by the Portuguese, and drove them with irresistible force from the crest of the position down the precipice. The 74th then advanced with the 9th, and kept up a fire upon the enemy as long as they could be reached. This attack, upon which the enemy had chiefly relied, having been thus repulsed, as well as those made by them upon the left of the Allied position, the fate of the day was finally decided, and they desisted from further efforts, after sustaining a loss of above 5,000 men killed and wounded.

★★★★★★

As different accounts have been frequently given regarding this part of the battle, a statement by Lieut. White (late Town-Major of Portsmouth), who was present in the battle as adjutant, and was stationed on the left and in rear of the regiment, of the occurrences which he personally observed is given in the Appendix, No. 7.

★★★★★★

Recollections of the Peninsula.

By the author of *Sketches in India*, 1825, Longman. (He was in Leith's Division.)

About this time, Lord Wellington, with a numerous staff, galloped up, and delivered his orders to General Hill, immediately in front of our corps (we were halted exactly in rear of that spot, from which the 74th Regiment, having just repulsed a column, was retiring in line, with the most beautiful regularity, its colours all torn with shot), I therefore distinctly heard him say:

'If they attempt this point again, Hill, you will give them a volley, and charge bayonets: but don't let your people follow them too far down the hill.'

Note.—The 74th Regiment had just been assisting by their fire to drive away the troops under Foy, who had just been charged by the 9th British Regiment.

No. 7.

Statement by Town-Major White, dated "Portsmouth, 6th July, 1848," of the occurrences observed by him, as Lieutenant and Adjutant of the 74th, at the Battle of Busaco.

At the Battle of Busaco the 74th were stationed, together with two field-pieces, under Major Arentschildt, of the Portuguese service, across a road leading over the mountain; the guns did much destruction to the enemy, and the fire which they drew in return did much execution in the ranks of the 74th Regiment without its fire being able to reach the enemy in retaliation.

Various desperate attacks were made by them (the enemy) to carry the hill in several places, but failed, as we witnessed, with much anxiety, until the afternoon, when they advanced more determinedly and with greater numbers, to force the road which the 74th protected, and it appeared we were by no means in numbers to resist them; a space being vacated on our left by a Portuguese regiment made our situation very desperate, which, it appears, was observed by the 5th Division from a distant height, and Gen. Leith sent two regiments with yellow facings (I think the 9th and 38th) to meet the enemy in this gap; they came at double-quick time along our rear from the right, and wheeled round in close column on our left, meeting the head of a mass of the French in close contact, who were advancing up the hill and likely to turn our left.

This contact was so immediate, and the hill so steep, that the brigade of the 5th Division had not time to deploy, but literally ran down upon the enemy in close column, or nearly so, the 74th moving forward with them part of the way; this decided the fate of the day, for the enemy never advanced afterwards. I mention this, because I have somewhere read that the 3rd Division was giving way when the 5th Division came down; this was not the case, the 74th never retreated a step the whole day, but advanced at last as above stated. I was near the

214

left of the regiment at the moment the brigade of the 5th Division arrived, and from the smoke and confusion I think the movement has not been clearly noticed by many besides myself, as I have frequently spoken to officers about it, who I found had not observed it. The brigade of the 5th Division came so hurriedly into action that they did not observe our position, and we, with an enemy forcing our front, did not observe them.

Capt. Carr Gomm, 1st November, 1810, to Major Henry Gomm.

I had not been six hours in Thomar when the order arrived for the immediate march of the division towards the Mondego. We marched immediately, crossing the river at Pena Cova, and took up our position in the line upon the Sierra of Busaco, and were not suffered to remain idle on the day the French attempted to force us.

We had at this time in our division the Brigade of the 9th, 38th, and Royals, the Lusitanian Legion, and 8th Portuguese, and the Brigade of the 3rd, 15th Portuguese, and Thomar Militia.

The British Brigade and the 8th were particularly called upon. The latter have had ample justice done them in the despatches, and they really deserve all that has been said of them, but you will not be able to judge of the merits of the 9th without a more detailed account than the despatches give of their feats.

The British Brigade was ordered up to the support of Gen. Picton, who sustained the left attack of the French. The brigade was marching left in front, so that the 9th led.

They passed in rear of Gen. Picton's right and centre, which was doing well; but on his left when the 9th Portuguese Regiment of his division, and the 8th of ours, had for some time withstood the attack of the French with great constancy, the enemy still continued to push up the hill, and when the head of our column arrived, marching rapidly behind the ridge of the hill, the Portuguese regiments were in some disorder, and the French were crowning the top of the hill to some extent, and increasing in numbers every instant. Gen. Leith was now at the head of the column which was at this moment showing its flank to the French, but it was necessary to keep marching to the front till we arrived opposite a space where the ascent was practicable (for the ridge was so rugged that in many parts it was not to be mounted without climbing), and wheeling into line we stood opposite to the French, at the distance of ten yards.

Both sides fired, and the 9th, being directed to charge, pushed over

215

the ridge, and all the Frenchmen who waited for them, and drove the remainder at a canter down the hill.

The 38th got a partial slap at them, but the Royals were not engaged.

I assure you we arrived in good time to do this, for they were improving their advantage rapidly: and on both sides of the breach they made, the alarm was spreading that they had turned us, so that our good fortune gave us an opportunity of repairing the state of affairs in this quarter at least, and it was the work of a few minutes.

Sir William Maynard Gomm at Busaco (Capt. Gomm of 9th Regiment). Letter of 1st November, 1810.

The 9th are out of humour with the despatches. They will have it that they did not *assist* in driving the enemy from the heights, nor had the 38th and Royals an opportunity of doing as they did: but according to their own story they found the French crowning the top of the hill after having driven away whatever had been opposed to them, waving their caps with exultation and increasing in number every instant: they climbed up at them and hurried them down the hill one over the other, while the alarm was spreading to the right and left that the French had succeeded in breaking through our line.

This, you see, was a good moment to arrive, but I can promise you that, if we had arrived a little later, our praises would have sounded louder, and what was really the work of ten minutes might in that case have been the labour of half, or many hours, or it might not have been done at all. This is the way the 9th tell their story, and I promise you it is a true one.

Extracts from Supplementary Despatches of Field-Marshal the Duke of Wellington.
Major-Gen. Picton to Lt.-Gen. Viscount Wellington.

Cadaceira, 10th Nov., 1810.

My Lord,

In consequence of an extraordinary report (see *Memoirs of Lieut.-General Sir T. Picton*, by H. B. Robinson, vol. 1), which has been circulated with a great deal of assiduity, it becomes necessary that I should make a written detailed report to your Lordship of the circumstances which preceded and attended the action which took place upon the heights of Busaco on the morning of the 27th September, inasmuch as they relate to myself and the troops I had the honour of commanding on that occasion.

Major-Gen. Lightburne, with the 5th and 83rd Regiments, was detached to the left, and did not act under my orders.

On the evening of the 25th, by orders from your Lordship, I occupied that part of the Serra de Busaco which is immediately connected with the pass of S. Antonio do Cantaro with Col. Mackinnon's Brigade, consisting of the 45th, 74th, and 88th Regiments, amounting to about 1,300 rank and file, and with the 9th and 21st Regiments of Portuguese infantry under Col. de Champelmond: upon the whole about 3,000 men.

All the movements of the enemy during the 26th indicating a determination of attacking the position early on the following morning, I made what dispositions I judged necessary for the defence of the post that evening; and there being an unoccupied space of considerably above a mile between my left and the right of Sir Brent Spencer's Division, immediately after sunset, when it could not be observed by the enemy, I detached Lt.-Col. Wallace with the 88th Regiment to take up an intermediate position and communicate with the hill of Busaco and the main body of my division at the pass of S. Antonio.

The troops in the immediate neighbourhood of the pass were visited by me on their respective posts before daybreak, and immediately after Col. Mackinnon returned from visiting the 88th Regiment, and reported that the enemy was collecting in the ravine opposite the position occupied by that regiment, in consequence of which I immediately detached Major Gwynne, of the 45th Regiment, with four companies to reinforce that post. A few minutes after, when the day began to clear up, a smart firing of musketry was heard on the left, apparently proceeding from the point where the 88th had been stationed; and after a short suspense a violent cannonade opened upon the pass of S. Antonio, and at the same time a heavy column compelled the advanced pickets of the division to fall back, and, pressing forward with great impetuosity, endeavoured to push up the road and force the pass. The light corps of the division, unable to resist such a superiority of numbers in front, was most judiciously thrown in upon the flank of the advancing column by Lt.-Col. Williams; and it was received with so steady and well-directed a fire by the 21st Portuguese Regiment of the line and three companies of the 74th that moved up to their support on the

217

left, that after a long struggle and repeated desperate attempts to effect their object (during which they suffered much from the well-directed fire of the Portuguese artillery under Major Arentschildt), they were ultimately under the necessity of desisting, though a severe firing of cannon and musketry still continued.

About this period, the fire of musketry on the left appearing to increase and draw nearer, I directed Col. Mackinnon to take the immediate command of the troops at the pass of S. Antonio, and rode towards the left, with the Assistant Adjutant-General, Major Pakenham, leaving my *aide-de-camp*, Capt. Cuthbert, and the Assistant Quartermaster-General, Capt. Anderson, to bring up as fast as possible one battalion of the 8th Portuguese Regiment, and the five remaining companies of the 45th Regiment. On reaching the high rocky point about half-way between the pass of S. Antonio and the hill of Busaco, I found the light companies of the 74th and 88th Regiments retiring in disorder, and the head of the enemy's column, already in possession of the strong rocky point, deliberately firing down upon us, and the remainder of a large column pushing up the hill with great rapidity. Whilst endeavouring to rally the light infantry companies with the assistance of Major Pakenham, I was joined by Major Smith of the 45th Regiment; and we succeeded in forming them under the immediate fire of the enemy, not more than sixty yards distant.

Major Smith most gallantly led them to the charge, and gained possession of the rock, driving the enemy before him; but I am concerned to say, fell in the moment of victory, for which we were chiefly indebted to his animating example. The Assistant Quartermaster-General having fortunately brought up a battalion of the 8th Portuguese Regiment, commanded by Major Birmingham, at this critical period, I personally led and directed their attack on the flank of the enemy's column; and we completely succeeded in driving them in great confusion and disorder down the hill and across the ravine.

Not being able to discover any enemy upon the ridge to my left, I immediately returned to the pass of S. Antonio, where the firing of musketry and cannon still continued with little apparent abatement. On my arrival I learned from Col. Mackinnon that the enemy had not been able to make any impression during my absence.

At this moment Major-Gen. Leith's *aide-de-camp* came to report the arrival of that general and his division, upon which I rode from the post of S. Antonio to the road of communication, and directed the leading regiment of the brigade to proceed without loss of time to the left, as I had no occasion for assistance. Gen. Leith's Brigade in consequence marched on, and arrived in time to join the five companies of the 45th Regiment under the Hon. Lt.-Col. Meade, and the 8th Portuguese Regiment under Lt.-Col. Douglas, in repulsing the last attempt of the enemy.

Your Lordship was pleased to mention me as directing the gallant charge of the 45th and 88th Regiments; but I can claim no merit whatever in the executive part of that brilliant exploit which your Lordship has so highly and so justly extolled. Lt.-Col. Wallace of the 88th, and Major Gwynne, who commanded the four companies of the 45th, and were, therefore, engaged on that occasion, are entitled to the whole of the merit, and I am not disposed to deprive them of any part. I was actively engaged at the time in repelling the attack upon the post with which I was principally charged, though I provided, as far as the means I had at my disposal would allow, for the safety of every part of the position within my reach; and the moment I could, with propriety and safety to the service, quit the principal point of my command, I immediately proceeded to the post where my services were most necessary, and was at all times to be found where His Majesty's service and my own honour required that I should be. I shall not say anything of the conduct of the troops under my command during the whole of the trying service of the day: it was beyond eulogy, and can receive no additional splendour from my feeble praise.

With many apologies for troubling your Lordship with such long details, in which I am necessarily so much concerned,

I have the honour to be, with high respect,

Your Lordship's very faithful humble servant,

Thos. Picton, Major-Gen.,

Commanding 3rd Division.

Major-Gen. Leith to Lt.-Gen. Viscount Wellington.

Camp of Sobral, 10th Nov., 1810.

As your important duty as Commander-in-Chief rendered it impossible that you should have witnessed all the movements made in an extensive line, of which various parts were engaged with the enemy at the same time, and as I apprehend that the principal effort made by my corps in the action of Busaco could not have come under your Lordship's personal observation, I submit to your consideration a report of the movements of the whole, and of the attack made on the enemy by part of the force under my command on the 27th of September.

The feeling which ought to have made me more delicate in touching on a subject where I happened to be personally concerned has been removed by your Lordship's having done me the honour already to mention my name in your public despatch. I have, therefore, no hesitation in fulfilling the gratifying duty of laying before you a report of the gallant and honourable manner in which those under my immediate command conducted themselves on one of the memorable occasions which mark your Lordship's military life.

I have the honour to be, my Lord,

Your most faithful and obedient servant,

James Leith, Major-Gen.

Report of the Position and Movements of Major-Gen. Leith's Corps, particularly of the British Brigade, during the Battle of Busaco, on the 27th of September, 1810.

At daybreak Major-Gen. Leith's Corps found itself posted as follows: the British Brigade, under Lt.-Col. Barnes; Royal, consisting of the 3rd Battalion Royal; 1st Battalion, 9th; and 2nd Battalion, 38th Regiments, were behind the ridge where the high roads from Gondolem and Carvalhos meet and cross the Serra do Busaco as one. At this point, and commanding the passage of the Serra, were placed four guns of the 6-pounder brigade of Portuguese artillery. In pursuance of directions received from Lord Wellington on the 26th, Brig.-Gen. Spry had moved from this point with his Portuguese Brigade, consisting of the 3rd Regiment, two battalions; the 15th *ditto, ditto*; and the Thomar Militia; the 8th Portuguese Regiment, two battalions, were likewise attached to him. They moved by their left till the leading regiment (the 8th) had nearly formed a junction with the right of Major-Gen. Picton's Division, posted to command near the high road leading across the Serra from S. Antonio do Cantaro. The two battalions of the Lusitanian Legion, under Col. Baron Eben, were posted about half distance between the British Brigade and Brig.-Gen. Spry. Two

6-pounders and 300 of the Lusitanian Legion, under Major Fearon, were posted in the redoubt of the chapel of N.S. de Monte Alto, on the right of the whole line.

The firing, which commenced towards the centre and left soon after daybreak, seemed to indicate a serious attack before 6 a.m.; that nearest on the left appeared principally directed against the position of S. Antonio do Cantaro, occupied by the 3rd Division. Lord Wellington had generally directed, on taking up the position, that the divisions should, in case of necessity, mutually support each other: finding there was no attack on his right or front, Major-Gen. Leith immediately put the brigades of his corps in motion by their left, the 6-pounder Portuguese artillery moving with the British Brigade. During this movement Major-Gen. Leith received a pencil note from Lord Wellington, which he communicated to Lt.-Gen. Hill, directing that he should move to his left, to support Major-Gen. Picton, unless Lt.-Gen. Hill's position on his right, or his own front, were attacked; to which the MajorGeneral replied that no attack was made or threatened, and that his corps had already been put in motion by its left for that purpose. Major-Gen. Leith rode on to ascertain the nature of the attack, and arrived at a commanding part of the Serra, where some Portuguese guns were posted on Major-Gen. Picton's right, and were firing on the road which passes over the Serra from S. Antonio do Cantaro, near which the enemy were endeavouring to ascend.

The ammunition of these guns being expended, and it being of much importance to have artillery at that point, Major-Gen. Leith immediately ordered the 6-pounder brigade of his corps to be placed there as soon as possible, which was accordingly done. Brig.-Gen. Spry's brigade and one battalion of the 8th Portuguese Regiment under Lt.-Col. Douglas, were in line in front of the rocky ridge near those guns, on both of which the enemy kept up a heavy cannonade, and succeeded in dismounting two of the guns, and wounding some officers and men. The 9th Portuguese Regiment, under the command of Lt.-Col. Sutton (belonging to Major-Gen. Picton's division), was also in line there.

The enemy, who was sometimes driven back and sometimes driving our troops, had, in conformity to his usual custom, a succession of columns to support the attack on Major-Gen. Picton's position, and now appeared evidently to gain ground on the face of the Serra to the left of the road of S. Antonio do Cantaro: Major-Gen. Leith accordingly directed a movement of succession, ordering Lt.-Col. Douglas, with the right battalion 8th Portuguese Regiment, to move by his left, to support the point attacked; he also ordered the 9th Portuguese Regiment, under Lt.-Col. Sutton (belonging to Major-Gen. Picton's division), to move to the support of Gen. Picton's position; and Brig.-Gen. Spry's Brigade was also ordered to move to its left, partly as a reserve and to support the Portuguese artillery under Major Arentschildt, near the road of S. Antonio do Cantaro.

The enemy during this movement disengaged part of his leading column, and branched into two, the first continuing to its right, the head of the second pointing towards its left, and threatening the position on the right of the road from S. Antonio do Cantaro, which caused Brig.-Gen. Spry's Brigade to be formed: this column, however, when the first column had succeeded, turned towards its right also, and followed the other, which was gaining the ascent of the Serra. The enemy was still advancing and had every appearance of succeeding in forcing that part of Major-Gen. Picton's position which is on the left of the road of S. Antonio do Cantaro, where several rocky eminences crown the ridge of the Serra.

Major-Gen. Leith, who had directed the British Brigade and Lusitanian Legion to move by the road of communication in rear of and nearly parallel to the ridge of the Serra, till it should appear where their support might be most necessary, now ordered the Lusitanian Legion to remain in column behind that part of the ridge which concealed its movements and those of the British Brigade from the view of the enemy, with its head resting so as to be ready to support, near the road, the Portuguese artillery under Major Arentschildt, and the 8th and 9th Portuguese Regiments, which he had ordered (as before stated) to support the point attacked, and where the enemy were fast gaining ground, while Major-Gen. Leith led the British Brigade by the shortest line to where it was evident their support was become essentially necessary.

The ground where the British Brigade was now moving behind a chain of rocky eminences, where it had appeared clearly the enemy was successfully pushing to establish himself, precluded Major-Gen. Leith from seeing at that moment the progress the enemy was making; but by the information of staff-officers stationed on purpose, who communicated his direction and progress. Major-Gen. Leith moved the British Brigade so as to endeavour to meet and check the enemy where he had gained the ascendancy. At this time a heavy fire of musketry was kept up on the height, the smoke of which prevented a clear view of the state of things. When, however, the rock forming the high part of the Serra, where Major-Gen. Picton's division was originally, became visible, the enemy appeared in full possession of it, and a French officer was in the act of cheering, with his hat off, while a continued fire was kept up from thence and along the whole face of the slope of the Serra, in a diagonal direction towards the bottom, by the enemy (ascending rapidly from the successive columns formed for the attack) on a mass of soldiers of the left battalion of the 8th and 9th Portuguese Regiments, who, having been severely pressed, had given way, and were rapidly retiring in complete confusion and disorder.

Major-Gen. Leith, on that occasion, spoke to Major Birmingham (who was on foot, having had his horse killed), who stated that the fugitives were of the 9th as well as of the 8th Regiment, and that he had ineffectually tried to check their retreat. Major-Gen. Leith addressed and succeeded in stopping them, and they cheered when he ordered them to be collected and formed in the rear. They were passing, as they retired, diagonally to the right of the 9th British Regiment. The face of affairs in this quarter now wore a different aspect, for the enemy, who had been the assailant, having dispersed or driven everything there opposed to him, was in possession of the rocky eminence of the Serra at this part of Major-Gen. Picton's position, without a shot being then fired at him.

Not a moment was to be lost. Major-Gen. Leith accordingly resolved instantly to attack the enemy with the bayonet; he therefore ordered the 9th British Regiment, which had been hitherto moving rapidly by its left in column (in order to gain the most advantageous ground for checking the enemy), to form the line, which they did with the greatest promptitude, accuracy, and coolness, under the fire of the enemy, who had just appeared formed on that part of the rocky eminence which overlooks the back of the ridge, and who had then, for the first time, also perceived the British Brigade under him.

Major-Gen. Leith had intended that the 38th Regiment should have moved on in rear and to the left of the 9th Regiment, to have turned the enemy beyond the rocky eminence, which was quite inaccessible towards the rear of the Serra, while the 9th should have gained the ridge on the right of the rocky height; the Royal to have been posted, as they were, in reserve; but the enemy, having driven everything before him in that quarter, afforded him the advantage of gaining the top of the rocky ridge, which is accessible in front, before it was possible for the British Brigade to reach that position, although not a moment had been lost in marching to support the point attacked, and for that purpose it had made a rapid movement of more than two miles without halting, and frequently in double-quick time. The 38th Regiment were therefore directed to form also and support, when Major-Gen. Leith had the honour to lead the 9th Regiment to attack the enemy on the rocky ridge, which they did without firing a shot.

That part which looks behind the Serra (as already stated) was inaccessible, and afforded the enemy the advantage of outflanking the 9th on the left as they advanced; but the order, celerity, and coolness with which they attacked, panic-struck the enemy, who immediately gave way on being charged with the bayonet, and the whole were driven down the face of the Serra in confusion and with immense loss, from a destructive fire which the 9th Regiment opened on him as he fled with precipitation after the charge. The 38th Regiment advanced with great coolness and spirit under a heavy fire to support the 9th while they were ascending to attack the enemy on the top of the rocky ridge, and, after the charge, they moved up on the right of the 9th and joined in the destructive pursuit of the enemy till the whole were ordered back, the action having entirely ceased after this, excepting a cannonade.

The steadiness and accuracy with which the 9th Regiment altered the direction of march, which, before they were engaged, was continually changing in order to form in the most advantageous manner for the attack of the enemy, the quickness and precision with which they formed line under a heavy fire, their instantaneous and orderly charge, by which they drove the enemy, so much superior in numbers, from a formidable position, and the promptitude with which they obeyed Major-Gen. Leith's order to cease firing, in his humble opinion was altogether conduct as distinguished as any regiment could have shown, and perhaps not the less worthy of notice that it is well known the attack was made by the flower of Regnier's corps, who had volunteered the service in which the enemy was then ultimately defeated.

Lt.-Col. Barnes, commanding the British Brigade, with great zeal and gallantry accompanied the 9th Regiment, which was commanded by Lt.-Col. Cameron, who, notwithstanding his being extremely ill, exerted himself with the greatest gallantry in front during the charge, when his horse was killed under him, Lt.-Col. Craufurd, who had been on duty during the night with the pickets, by a zealous exertion arrived in time also to distinguish himself in front of his regiment. Lt.-Col. Nugent, commanding, Major Loftus, and the 2nd Battalion 38th

Regiment evinced the greatest coolness and spirit while they were engaged with the enemy; the 3rd Battalion Royals, commanded by Major Gordon (an excellent officer), although they had not the good fortune to be actively engaged, showed great zeal, coolness, and order in crossing the fire of the enemy's cannon.

Major-Gen. Leith cannot close this report without stating the zeal, activity, and gallantry of Major Berkeley, 35th Regiment, Assistant Adjutant-General; Capt. Gomm, 9th Regiment, Deputy Assistant Quartermaster-General; and Capts. Hare, 23rd, and Sutton, 97th, who voluntarily assisted in the Adjutant and Quartermaster-General's department, and Lieut. Leith Hay, 29th Regiment, his *aide-de-camp*; all these officers distinguished themselves on horseback in front of the 9th Regiment during the charge, as did also Lieut. Oliviera of the Lusitanian Legion, who was attached to Major-Gen. Leith's corps.

James Leith, Major-Gen.

Extracts from Major-Gen. Sir John Cameron's Letters to Col. Napier.

Government House, Devonport,
Aug. 9th, 1834.

I am sorry to perceive in the recent publication of Lord Beresford, his "*Refutation of your Justification of your third volume*" some remarks on the battle of Busaco which disfigure, not intentionally I should hope, the operations of the British Brigade in Major-Gen. Leith's corps on that occasion, of which I, as commanding officer of one of the regiments composing it, may perhaps be permitted to know something. I shall, however, content myself at present with giving you a detail of the operations of the British Brigade in Major-Gen. Leith's *own words,* extracted from a document in my possession, every syllable of which can be verified by many distinguished officers now living, some of them actors in, all of them eye-witnesses to, the affair.

"The ground where the British Brigade was now moving," etc. Then follows long extract from above letter to Wellington.

I shall merely add two observations on what has been asserted in the *Refutation.*

First, with regard to the confusion and retreat of a portion of the Portuguese troops, I certainly did not know at the moment what Portuguese corps the fugitives were of, but after the action I understood they were belonging to the 8th Portuguese; a very considerable number of them were crossing the front of the British column dispersed in sixes and sevens over the field just before I wheeled the 9th Regiment into line for the attack. I pushed on a few yards to entreat them to keep out of our way, which they understood and called out, "*Viva los Ingleses, valerosos Portugueses.*"

As regards any support which the Portuguese afforded the British Brigade in the pursuit, I beg to say that during the charge, while leading the regiment in front of the centre, my horse was killed under me, which for a moment retarded my own personal advance, and on extricating myself from under him, I turned round and saw the 38th Regiment close up with us and the Royal Scots appearing over the ridge in support, but did not see any Portuguese join in the pursuit; indeed it would have been imprudent in them to attempt such a thing, for at the time a brisk cannonade was opened upon us from the opposite side of the ravine.

This, my dear colonel, is, on my honour, an account of the operations of the British Brigade in Major-Gen. Leith's corps at Busaco. It will be satisfactory to you to know that the information you received has been correct. The anonymous officer of the 9th Regiment I do not know. There were several very capable of furnishing you with good information on the transactions of that day, not only as regarded their own immediate corps, but those around them. Col. Waller I should consider excellent authority; that gallant officer must have been an eye-witness to all that passed in the divisions of Picton and Leith. I remember on our approach to the scene of confusion he delivered me a message from Gen. Picton, intended for Gen. Leith, at the time reconnoitring, to hasten our advance.

GOVERNMENT HOUSE, DEVONPORT,

Aug. 21st, 1834.

. . . The fact really is that both the 8th and 9th Portuguese Regiments gave way that morning, and I am positive that I am not far wrong in saying, that there were not of Portuguese troops within my view, at the moment I wheeled the 9th Regiment into line, one hundred men prepared either for attack or defence. Sir James Douglas partly admits that his wing was broken when he says that "if we were at any time *broken* it was from the too ardent wish of a corps of boy recruits to close." Now it is perfectly clear that the wing of the regiment under Major Birmingham fled, from what that officer said to General Leith. Sir James Douglas states also that "no candid man will deny that he supported the Royals and 9th Regiment," though before that he says, that "by an oblique movement he joined in the charge." I might safely declare on oath that the Portuguese never showed themselves beyond the ridge of the Serra that morning.

Very faithfully yours,

John Cameron.

Extract from memorandum of the Battle of Busaco, by Colonel Waller, Assistant Quartermaster -General to the 2nd Division.

The attack commenced on the right wing, consisting of Picton's Division, by the enemy opening a fire of artillery upon the right of the British which did but little injury, the range being too great to prove effective. At this moment were seen the heads of the several attacking columns, three, I think, in number, and deploying into line with the most beautiful precision, celerity, and gallantry.

As they formed on the plateau they were cannonaded from our position, and the regiment of Portuguese, either the 8th or the 16th *Infantry*, which were formed in advance in *front* of the 74th *Regiment*, threw in some volleys of musketry into the enemy's columns in a flank direction, but the regiment was quickly driven into the position.

More *undaunted* courage never was displayed by *French* troops than on *this* occasion, it could not have been surpassed; for their columns advanced in despite of a tremendous fire of grape and musketry from our troops in position in the rocks, and overcoming all opposition although repeatedly charged by Lightburne's Brigade, or rather by the whole of Picton's division, they advanced, and fairly drove the British right wing from the rocky part of the position.

Being an eye-witness of this critical moment, and seeing that unless the ground was quickly recovered *the right flank* of the army would *infallibly* be turned, and the *great road* to Coimbra *unmasked*, seeing also that heavy columns of the enemy were descending into the valley to operate by the *road*, and to support the attack of the Sierra, and to cut off Lord Wellington's communication with Coimbra, I instantly galloped off to the rear to bring up Gen. Hill's Corps to Picton's support. Having proceeded about *two* miles along the upper edge and reverse side of the Sierra, I fell in with the head of Gen. Leith's column moving *left in front*, at the head of which was Col. Cameron's Brigade, led by the 9th Regiment. I immediately rode up to Col. Cameron, and addressed him in an anxious tone as follows:

"Pray, sir, who commands this brigade?"—"I do," replied the colonel, "I am Colonel Cameron."

"Then for God's sake, sir, move off instantly at *double-quick* with your brigade to Picton's support not one moment is to be lost, the enemy in great force are already in possession of the *right of the position* on the Sierra and have driven Picton's troops out of it. Move on, and when the rear of your brigade has passed the Coimbra road wheel into line, and you will embrace the point of attack." Col. Cameron did not hesitate *or balance* an instant, but giving the word double-quick to his brigade, nobly led them to battle and to victory.

The brave colonel attacked the enemy with such a gallant and irresistible impetuosity, that after some time fighting, he recovered the ground which Picton had lost, inflicting *heavy slaughter* on the *élite* of the enemy's troops. The 9th Regiment behaved on this occasion with conspicuous gallantry, as *indeed* did all the regiments engaged. Great numbers of the enemy had descended low down in the rear of the position towards the Coimbra road, and were killed; the whole position was thickly strewed with their killed and wounded, amongst which *were many of our own troops*. The French were the finest men I ever saw. I spoke to several of the wounded men, light infantry and grenadiers, who were bewailing their unhappy fate on being defeated, assuring me they were the heroes of Austerlitz, who had never before met with Defeat!

Robert Waller, Lieut.-Col.

Extract of a Letter from Col. Taylor, 9th Regiment, to Col. Napier.

Fernhill, near Evesham,
26th April, 1832.

I have just received a letter from Col. Shaw, in which he quotes a passage from one of yours to him, expressive of your wish, if necessary, to print a passage from a statement which I made respecting the conduct of the 9th Regiment at Busaco, and in reference to which, I have alluded to the discomfiture of the 8th Portuguese upon the same occasion. I do not exactly recollect the terms I made use of to Col. Shaw (nor indeed the shape which my communication wore), but my object was to bring to light the distinguished conduct of the 9th without any wish to unnecessarily obscure laurels which others wore, even at their expense!

To account for the affair in question, I could not, however, well omit to state, that it was in consequence of the overthrow of the 8th Portuguese that Sir James Leith's British Brigade was called upon, and it is remarkable that, at the time, there was a considerable force of Portuguese (I think it was the old Lusitanian Legion, which had just been modelled into two battalions) *between* Leith's British and where the 8th were being engaged. Leith pushed on his brigade double-quick, column of sections left in front, past these Portuguese, nor did he halt until he came in contact with the enemy, who had *crowned the heights* and were firing from behind the rocks.

The 9th wheeled up into line, fired and charged, and all of the 8th Portuguese that was to be seen, at least by me, a company officer at the time, was some ten or a dozen men at *the outside*, with their commanding officer; but he and they were amongst the very foremost in the ranks of the 9th British. As an officer in the ranks, of course, I could not see much of what was going on generally, neither could I well have been mistaken as to what I did see, coming almost within my very contact! Col. Waller, now, I believe, on the Liverpool Staff, was the officer who came to Sir James Leith for assistance, I presume from Picton.

Yours, etc.,

J. Taylor.

Third Communication from Major-Gen. Sir John Cameron to Col. Napier.

Stoke, Devonport,
Nov. 21st, 1835.

My dear Colonel,

Some months ago I took the liberty of pointing out to you certain mis-statements contained in a publication of Lord Beresford regarding the operations of the British Brigade in Major-Gen. Leith's Corps at the battle of Busaco; and as those mis-statements are again brought before the public in Robinson's *Life of Sir Thomas Picton*, I am induced to trouble you with some remarks upon what is therein advanced. A paragraph in Major-Gen. Picton's letter to Lord Wellington, dated 10th November, 1810, which I first discovered some years ago in the Appendix, No. 12, of Jones's *War in Spain*, etc. etc., would appear to be the document upon which Mr. Robinson grounds his contradiction of your statement of the conduct of the 9th Regiment at Busaco; but that paragraph, which runs as follows, I am bound to say is not the truth. "Major-Gen. Leith's Brigade in consequence marched on, and arrived in time to join the five companies of the 45th Regiment under the honourable Lt.-Col. Meade, and the 8th Portuguese Regiment under Lt.-Col. Douglas, in repulsing the enemy."

This assertion of Major-Gen. Picton, is, I repeat, not true, for, in the first place, I did not see the 45th Regiment on that day, nor was I at any period during the action near them or any other British regiment to my left. In the second, as regards the 8th Portuguese Regiment, the 9th British did not most assuredly join that corps in its retrograde movement. That Major-Gen. Picton left his right flank exposed there can be no question, and had no assistance, and British assistance, come up to his aid as it did, I am inclined to believe that Sir Thomas would have cut a very different figure in the despatch to what he did!! Having already given you a detail of the defeat of the enemy's column, which was permitted to gain the ascendancy in considerable force on the right of the 3rd Division, I beg leave to refer you to the gallant officers I mentioned in a former letter, who were not only eye-witnesses to the charge made by the 9th Regiment, but actually distinguished themselves in front of the regiment, at the side of their brave accomplished general during that charge.

I believe the whole of Sir Rowland Hill's Division from a bend in the Sierra could see the 9th in their pursuit of the enemy, and though last not the least in importance, as a party concerned, I may mention the present Major-Gen. Sir James T. Barnes, who commanded the British Brigade under Major-Gen. Leith (I omitted this gallant officer's name in my former letter), as the Major-General took the entire command, and from him alone I received all orders during the action.

I have now done with Mr. Robinson and his work, which was perhaps hardly worth my notice.

> I am, my dear Colonel,
> Very sincerely yours,
>
> J. Cameron.

The casualties amongst British non-commissioned officers serving with Portuguese regiments are not on record, but there are a number of these included in the Portuguese returns.

Prof. Oman works out the losses of British and Portuguese at 626

RETURN OF BRITISH CASUALTIES, 25TH, 26TH, AND 27TH SEPTEMBER, 1810.

	OFFICERS.		MEN. (Including non-com.)			Total.
	Killed.	Wounded	Killed.	Wounded.	Missing.	
On 27th Sept.						
General Staff	—	4	—	—	—	4
British Horse Artillery	—	—	—	2	—	2
British Foot Artillery	—	—	1	5	—	6
General Foot Artillery	—	—	—	3	—	3
3rd Batt. 1st Foot	—	—	—	2	—	2
2nd „ 5th „	—	—	1	7	—	8
1st „ 7th „	—	1	1	22	—	24
1st „ 9th „	—	1	5	18	—	24
2nd „ 24th „	—	1	—	—	—	1
2nd „ 38th „	—	1	5	17	—	23
2nd „ 42nd „	—	—	—	6	—	6
1st „ 43rd „	—	—	—	8	—	8
1st „ 45th „	3	4	22	106	12	147
1st „ 50th „	—	1	—	—	—	1
1st „ 52nd „	—	3	3	10	—	16
5th „ 60th Rifles	—	5	3	16	5	29
1st „ 74th Foot	1	1	6	21	2	31
1st „ 79th „	1	1	7	41	6	56
2nd „ 83rd „	—	1	—	4	—	5
1st „ 88th „	1	8	30	94	1	134
1st „ 95th „	—	—	9	22	—	31
1st Line K.G.L.	—	1	3	5	—	9
Detachment K.G.L.	—	—	1	11	3	15
„ 2nd K.G.L.	—	1	1	6	—	8
2nd Batt. Line K.G.L.	—	1	3	6	1	11
5th „ „ „	—	—	1	9	—.	10
7th „ „ „	—	—	—	9	—	9
	6	35	102	450	30	623
Also on 25th, 26th Sept.						
14th Light Dragoons	—	—	—	3	3	6
16th „ „	—	1	—	—	4	5
1st Hussars K.G.L.	—	—	—	4	—	4
General Staff (Hoey)	—	1	—	—	—	1
	6	37	102	457	37	639
Add. British Officers serving with Portuguese regiments	3	5	—	—	—	8
	9	42	102	457	37	647
Portuguese losses	3	20	90*	487	20	620
Grand Total	12	62	192	944	57	1,267

* Doubtful : may be 84.

each, which he describes as "an extraordinary coincidence in the total losses of the two nations." There are various differences between the Professor's calculations and mine, which make the alleged coincidence more than doubtful.

Casualties on 25th and 26th Sept., 1810, while retiring and taking up position at Bussaco.

General Staff : 1 captain wounded severely—Capt. Hoey, D.A.A.G.

14th Light Dragoons : 1 sergeant, 2 rank and file wounded.

16th Light Dragoons : 1 cornet slightly wounded (Cornet Keating).

1st Hussars, K.G.L., 1 sergeant, 3 rank and file wounded.

Names of officers (British) killed and wounded at Bussaco.

Killed—With Portuguese regiments :

    Capt. W. McIntosh, of 4th British Foot, 1st Line.

    Capt. Charles Fox, of 2/66th British Foot, 16th Line.

    Capt. Salisbury, of British 62nd Foot, 21st Line.

With British troops :

    1/45th Foot : Major Smyth, Capt. Urquhart, Lt. Ouseley.

    74th Foot : Ensign Williams.

    1/79th Foot : Capt. A. Cameron.

    1/88th Foot : Lt. H. Johnson.

Wounded—With Portuguese regiments :

Major Prior, 1st Line.

Lt. V. Mathias, 8th Line.

Capt. S. Burgess, 21st Line.

Lt. J. Machell, 21st Line.

Capt. L. Homm, 6th Caçadores (possibly a German).

With British troops :

Unit	Name	Severity
General Staff	Lt.-Col. C. Campbell, 70th Foot, A.A.G.	Slightly
	Capt. Lord Fitzroy Somerset, 43rd Foot, A.D.C. to Lord Wellington	,,
	Capt. Marquis of Tweeddale, 1st Foot Guards, D.A.Q.M.G.	,,
	Capt. G. Preston, 1/40th Foot, A.D.C. to Sir B. Spencer	,,
1/7th Foot	Lt. Mair	,,
1/9th ,,	Lt. Lindsay	Severely
2/24th ,,	Capt. Meachan	Slightly
2/38th ,,	Lt. Miller	,,
1/45th ,,	Major Gwynne	Severely
	Lt. Harris	,,
	Lt. Tyler	,,
	Lt. Anderson	,,
1/50th	Major Napier	,,
1/52nd	Lt.-Col. Barclay (died at home of it)	Slightly
	Capt. G. Napier	,,
	Lt. C. Wood	,,
5/60th Rifles	Lt.-Col. Williams	,,
	Capt. Andrews	,,
	Lt. Josie, *or* Joice	Severely
	Lt. Eberstein	,,
	Lt. Franhein	,,
1/74th Foot	Lt. Cargill	Severely
1/79th ,,	Capt. Douglas	,,
2/83rd ,,	Lt. Colthurst	Slightly
1/88th ,,	Major Silver (since dead)	Severely
	Major McGregor	,,
	Capt. McDermot	,,
	Capt. Dansey	Slightly
	Capt. Bury	,,
	Lt. Fitzpatrick	Severely
	Lt. Nickle	,,
	Ensign Leonard	,,

1/K.G.L.	Lt. During	Slightly
2/K.G.L.	Major Wurmt	,,
Detachment 2nd Light K.G.L.	Lt. Stolte	Severely

PORTUGUESE CASUALTIES AT BUSSACO.

(Based on figures given by Prof. Oman and Lord Londonderry, and bulletins.)

	OFFICERS.		MEN.			Total.
	Killed.	Wounded	Killed.	Wounded.	Missing.	
9th Line . . .	—	1	5	23	—	29
21st Line . .	1	3	13	67	—	84
8th Line . . .	1	4	29	102	9	145
1st Caçadores . .	—	—	2	20	1	23
3rd ,, . .	—	3	10	76	—	89
1st Line . . .	—	2	4	32	—	38
16th Line . . .	—	2	2	26	2	32
4th Caçadores . .	1	4	9	52	—	66
7th Line . . .	—	—	—	3	—	3
19th Line . . .	—	1	8	28	—	37
2nd Caçadores . .	—	—	6	30	7	43
6th ,, . .	—	—	1	20	1	22
Artillery . . .	—	—	1	8	—	9
	3	20	90*	487	20	620

* Londonderry and bulletins say only 84 men killed. Oman gives 90, but does not give his authority. I accept the latter, as it is divided up amongst the regiments.

Portuguese Officers.

Killed :	Capt. de Souza	8th Line.
	Ensign Castes ,, das Novas Franci	4th Caçadores.
Wounded :	Ensign J. M. de Pantos ,, B. de Senio	1st Line.
	Capt. F. Auzabis Ensign J. A. Rodrigo ,, Manuel Pedro ,, J. Manuel	8th Line.
	,, Felix Antonio	9th Line.
	Capt. P. Joccé Ensign J. Maria	16th Line.
	Lieut. J. Galderio	19th Line.
	Col. de Champalimaud Ensign J. Montero ,, J. Alberto	21st Line.

234

„	Botello Cas	
„	Segurada	3rd Caçadores.
„	J. Chrostimo	
Capt.	J. Bernardo	
Lieut.	A. Queroz	
„	J. D. Vasconcella	4th Caçadores.
Ensign	Feliziamo	

★★★★★★

The names given in the official list of Portuguese officer casualties should probably have been:—

Santos	not	Pantos
Auzebio	"	Auzabis
Rodriques	"	Rodrigo
Monteiro	"	Montero
Chrisotismo	"	Chrostimo
Queiroz	"	Queroz
Vasconello	"	Vasconella
Feliciamo	"	Feliziamo.

★★★★★★

French Losses at Bussaco

Wellington (Despatch of 30th Sept., 1810), states that the French left 2,000 killed upon the field of battle, and that Gen. Simon, 3 colonels, and 250 men were taken prisoners—with an immense loss in wounded.

Napier says the French loss was preposterously exaggerated at the time, but it was really great—one General, Graindorge, and 800 men killed. The whole loss might be about 4,500.

The returns procured by Prof. Oman from the *Archives des Ministère de la Guerre* show:

Killed and prisoners	899
Wounded	3,580
Total	4,479

But the Professor points out various small discrepancies, and estimates the total at 4,600 killed, wounded and missing. There is a misprint "939" for "993" total men wounded in Marchand's Division.

Considerable numbers of badly wounded French were left behind by Masséna, owing to want of transport; but Trant captured at Coim-

235

bra, on the *7th September*, 3,507 sick and wounded (Oman), but Napier says 5,000 wounded and unwounded—besides 300 next day—which generally confirms the figures of the Archives as regards the wounded. But one cannot doubt that the French killed were 2,000, as Wellington reported, which makes the figures:

Killed	2,000
Prisoners	254
Wounded	3,580
	———
Total	5,834
	———

against estimates of 10,000 published in England at the time.

I am not prepared on the evidence to accept the records of casualties as recorded in the office of the French Minister of War—in the first place because Masséna deceived Napoleon, and secondly because Napoleon habitually caused false statements to be prepared of the losses of his armies. The only reliable documents were those prepared for himself, and even these were falsified by those wishing to deceive him, as Masséna undoubtedly did. However, I give the War Office figures as obtained by Prof. Oman.

They are probably too small. It would be interesting to know whether these returns of casualties were bound in yellow or green. In the case of Muster Rolls two sets were always prepared, one for the Emperor, and the other for the public records, and it is probable that the Returns of Casualties were treated similarly (*vide* Napier, Vol. 1).

2ND CORPS.	Killed or prisoners.		Wounded.		Total.
	Officers.	Men.	Officers.	Men.	
MERLE'S DIVISION :					
Sarrut's Brigade :					
2nd Léger	2	81	16	209	308
36th Ligne	6	178	22	277	483
Graindorge's Brigade :					
4th Léger	11	118	9	110	248
Artillery	—	—	—	2	2
Divisional Total	19	377	47	598	1,041
HEUDELET'S DIVISION :					
Foy's Brigade :					
17th Léger	2	60	20	271	353
70th Ligne	6	54	11	246	317
Arnaud's Brigade :					
31st Léger	3	67	7	219	296
47th Ligne	—	—	3	3	6
Artillery	—	—	—	6	6
Divisional Total	11	181	41	745	978

Corps Troops :					
Engineers	—	1	—	2	3
Train	—	1	—	—	1
Total	30	560	88	1,345	2,023

6TH CORPS.	Killed or prisoners.		Wounded.		Total.
	Officers.	Men.	Officers.	Men.	
MARCHAND'S DIVISION :					
Maucune's Brigade :					
6th Léger	2	70	12	281	365
69th Ligne	2	44	18	416	480
Marcognet's Brigade :					
39th Ligne	—	19	3	213	235
76th Ligne	—	7	3	83	93
Divisional Total	4	140	36	993	1,173
MERMET'S DIVISION :					
Bardet's Brigade :					
25th Léger	—	3	—	20	23
27th Ligne	—	—	1	—	1
Lebassée's Brigade :					
50th, 59th (no losses)	—	—	—	—	—
Divisional Total	—	3	1	20	24
LOISON'S DIVISION :					
Simon's Brigade :					
26th Ligne	6	37	15	225	283
Légion du Midi	1	32	5	273	311
Légion Hanovrienne	4	26	5	182	217
Ferey's Brigade :					
32nd Léger	2	13	3	95	113
66th Ligne	5	15	15	123	158
82nd Ligne	3	18	4	145	170
Divisional Total	21	141	47	1,043	1,252
ÉTAT-MAJOR :	—	—	7	—	7
Total	25	284	91	2,056	2,456
Grand Total	55	844	179	3,401	4,479

It is impossible to reconcile above statement of Loison's loss in " killed 162 " with the accounts of the terrible defeat Craufurd's Division inflicted on him—the guns alone must have killed more. And when it is remembered that the 162 includes prisoners the return seems altogether unreliable.

History of Worcestershire Regiment, May, 1811.

At this period there were about 47,000 French prisoners in England, while 10,300 languished in the prisons of France (*Chambers's Journal,* 1875, No. 607). Those on parole were often described as accomplished, amusing, and orderly in their behaviour.

A report laid before the House of Commons showed that in three years nearly 700 French officers and other persons broke their parole, five of whom were generals, but during the whole war only one Englishman broke his parole in France, and that one a very young midshipman in the navy.

In the condition of those prisoners who patiently kept their parole in the country towns in England, where they were stationed in parties of from 100 to 200, there was nothing offensive to the feelings, but what was truly revolting to every sense of propriety was the spectacle of vast groups of prisoners: 10,000 at Norman's Cross, thousands at Dartmoor, and so on, confined like wild beasts for years within palisade enclosures, and in a state of that utter idleness which led to criminal acts, as it were, to relieve the tedium of their dismal incarceration.

To Lt.-Gen. Hill.

Arruda, 8th Oct., 1810

Sir.

I request you also tomorrow morning to send a brigade of Portuguese 6-pounders (which you were to have sent to Gen. Leith in exchange for the 9pounders) and two 6-pounders belonging to the brigade with Major-Gen. Leith, which you brought for Nostra Senhora del Monte, from Villa Franca through Alhandra and Arruda to Solval, where the 6-pounder brigade is to join the 6th Division of Infantry. And the two 6-pounders are to be sent on to Ribaldeira to join the 3rd Division of Infantry.

I also request you to send from Villa Franca to Cabaça the Portuguese 9-pounder brigade which has been with your corps, where it is to remain a reserve.

The other Portuguese 6-pounder brigade with your corps, and the 3-pounder brigade with Col. Le Cor, must be brought to Alhandra.

Wellington.

The Napiers at Bussaco.

There were four Napiers at this battle:

(1) Captain George Napier, 52nd Regiment, who was wounded in the hip.

(2) Major Charles James Napier, a volunteer from the 50th Regiment, serving usually with the Light Division, but attached to Wellington's Staff during this battle.

(3) Capt. William Napier, 43rd Regiment, the historian of the

Peninsular War.

(4) Captain Charles Napier, afterwards an admiral, a cousin of the above three brothers, who was there as a spectator, and was slightly wounded in the leg on the previous day.

In his *Life of Charles James Napier*, by Lt.-Gen. Sir William Napier (No. 3) the following passage occurs:

Charles Napier (No. 2) clinging to the Light Division was engaged in all the skirmishes until the English general, halting on Bussaco Mountain, offered battle. There, riding in the train of Wellington, at the point where Reynier's troops assailed the position, he remained on horseback when the fire was so terrible that all the staff, and all the volunteers, with the exception of his cousin, the present Admiral Napier (No. 4), had dismounted. He, seeing the only man mounted in a red coat, when all the others were in blue, urged him to alight—at least to put on his cloak, or he would be marked down. His answer was, 'No, no. This is the uniform of my regiment, and in it I will shew, or fall this day.' Scarcely had the words been uttered than he fell. A bullet had entered on the right of his nose and lodged in the left jaw near the ear, shattering the bone in pieces. He was borne away past Lord Wellington, and though sinking from loss of blood, took off his hat and waved it, muttering, for he was unable to speak out, 'I could not die at a better moment.'

Such was Admiral Napier's account of the event, and he added, that holding him during the extraction of the ball, that fearful operation was treated as lightly as the drawing of a tooth would be. Apparently dying, he was now consigned to the Convent of Bussaco some miles off. His wound was then dressed, and he found his way to Coimbra, a day's march, by next morning. He hoped to have rest and care at that place, but was hardly able to preserve his life from the brutality and cowardice, if not worse, of an army physician, not a surgeon, to whom he had been delivered.

This vile fellow, becoming cognisant of a rumour that the enemy was approaching, not only left his hurts actually unbandaged to save himself, but carried off his patient's horses, leaving him for several hours in expectation of death, or captivity. His servant, an active fellow, recovered the animals by force, and bandaged his master's face again. Then he made his way on horseback, under a burning sun, to Lisbon—a journey of several days. The 50th Regiment, coming up to join the army, passed him on the road, and gave him three cheers; and at Lisbon he was joined by his brother George, who had been shot through the upper part of the thigh.

Asking for Promotion.

To the C. in C.

Sheweth:

That when your Memorialist was seven years a lieutenant you gave him an extra shilling. On the 16th of last September he was fourteen years a Lieutenant, and he hopes you will give him another extra shilling.

Your Memorialist has seen some service, having been present in 15 general engagements, 64 skirmishes, and 13 flying camps, and he further takes the liberty of hinting that he is the oldest subaltern in the world.

The Memorial of Kroppf Hoffmeyer.
1810.

BUSSACO

27ᵗʰ Sept 1810

Rough Plan of ground defended by
Gen R. Craufurd when attacked by
Loison's Division
(not to scale)

BRITISH

PORTUGUESE

FRENCH

FRENCH ATTACK

400 feet lower than the windmill is Sula villnum
on rising base - guns were trained
The main through to the villnum could not see
down by path's gate - so 95th could not see
much of the villnum coming to verge of hill side

From Sula to rocky ledge, 6 minutes to walk.
Rocky ledge to Windmill, one minute to walk.

Craufurd's rock

ledge of rocks B&MR drop

crest of hill

road of hill

Distance B to C
100 paces

D

To 52ⁿᵈ windmill, 87 paces

C

Gully runs from
gate to left

Windmill

52ⁿᵈ REG. 975 STRONG

43ᵈ REG. 844 STRONG

4 COˢ 95ᵀᴴ 370 STRONG

4 COˢ 95ᵀᴴ 296 STRONG

3ᵈ CAÇADORES 280 STRONG

3ᵈ CAÇADORES 826 STRONG

Old road to Sula & Mora

New road to Mora in cutting

To Coimbra

A

Distance A to E
by road 160 yards

KING'S GERMAN LEGION ABOUT A QUARTER OF A MILE
FURTHER TO THE REAR

6TH CORPS (JUNOT) IN RESERVE   CAVALRY IN RESERVE

REMMIS & COLLINS of COLE'S DIVISION
FURTHER TO LEFT (NOT SHOWN)

NEY'S CORPS
RESERVES   MERMET

Sula   *Moira*

Cerqueão

LOISON

N.G.L

Porta
da Rainha

to Coimbra

Porta
da Sula

BUSSACO
CONVENT

PACK

Road of Communication
PAKENHAM   14th Métres
                         CAMERON   (High ground)
                                         LIGHTBURN
                        STOPFORD

14TH
(2 SQUAD)

Ser

Scale in Yards   100 200 300 400 500   1000   1500 YARDS

BATTLE OF BUSSACO
Sep. 27th 1810.
EARLY IN THE MORNING

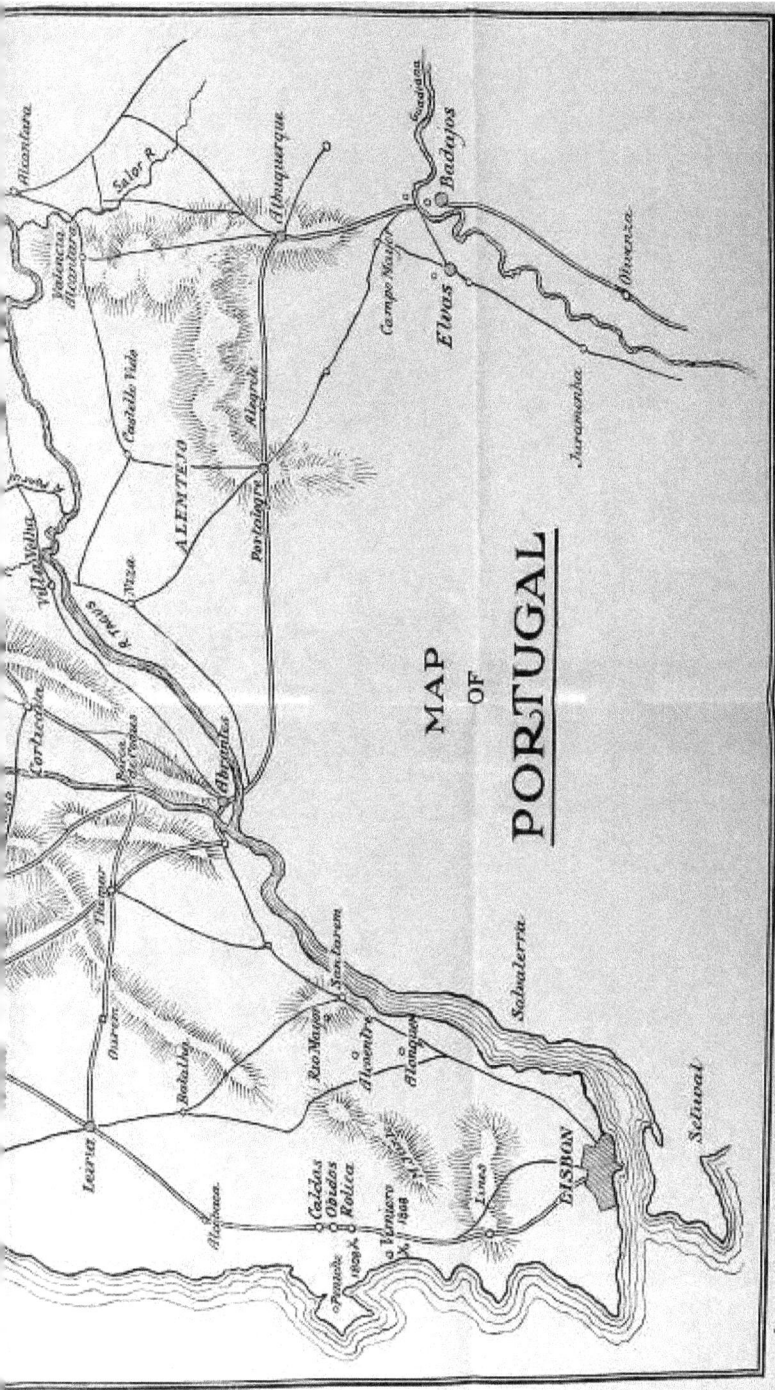

MAP

OF

PORTUGAL

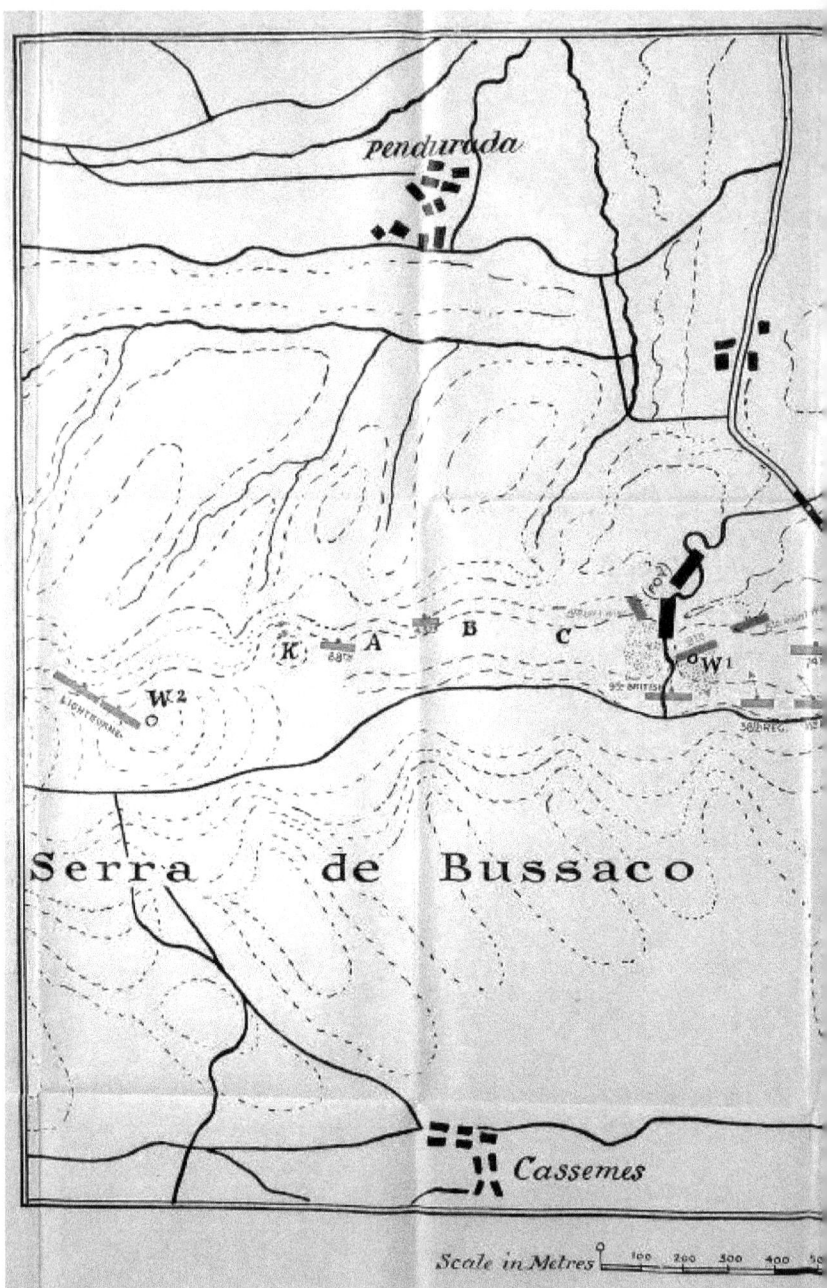

Penduroda

Serra de Bussaco

K A B C

W1

W2

LIGHTSNWE

95? BRITISH

50? REG.

Cassemes

Scale in Metres 100 200 300 400 50

BATTLE OF BUSSACO
Sep. 27th 1810.

2nd phase of Foy's attack.

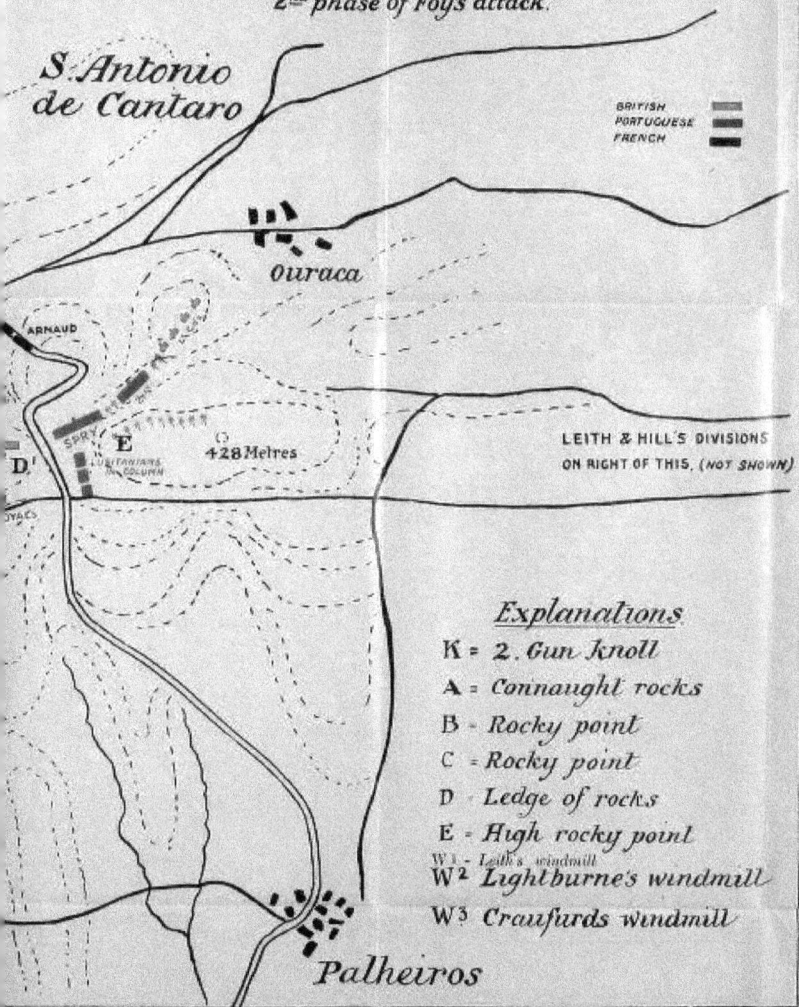

S. Antonio
de Cantaro

BRITISH
PORTUGUESE
FRENCH

Ouraca

ARNAUD

E

D'

G 428 Metres

SPRY

LUSITANIANS
IN COLUMN

OYA'CS

LEITH & HILL'S DIVISIONS
ON RIGHT OF THIS, (NOT SHOWN)

Explanations

K = 2. Gun Knoll
A = Connaught rocks
B = Rocky point
C = Rocky point
D = Ledge of rocks
E = High rocky point
W 1 = Leith's windmill
W 2 Lightburne's windmill
W 3 Craufurds windmill

Palheiros

SWAN SONNENSCHEIN & CO LTD LONDON

1000   1500 METRES

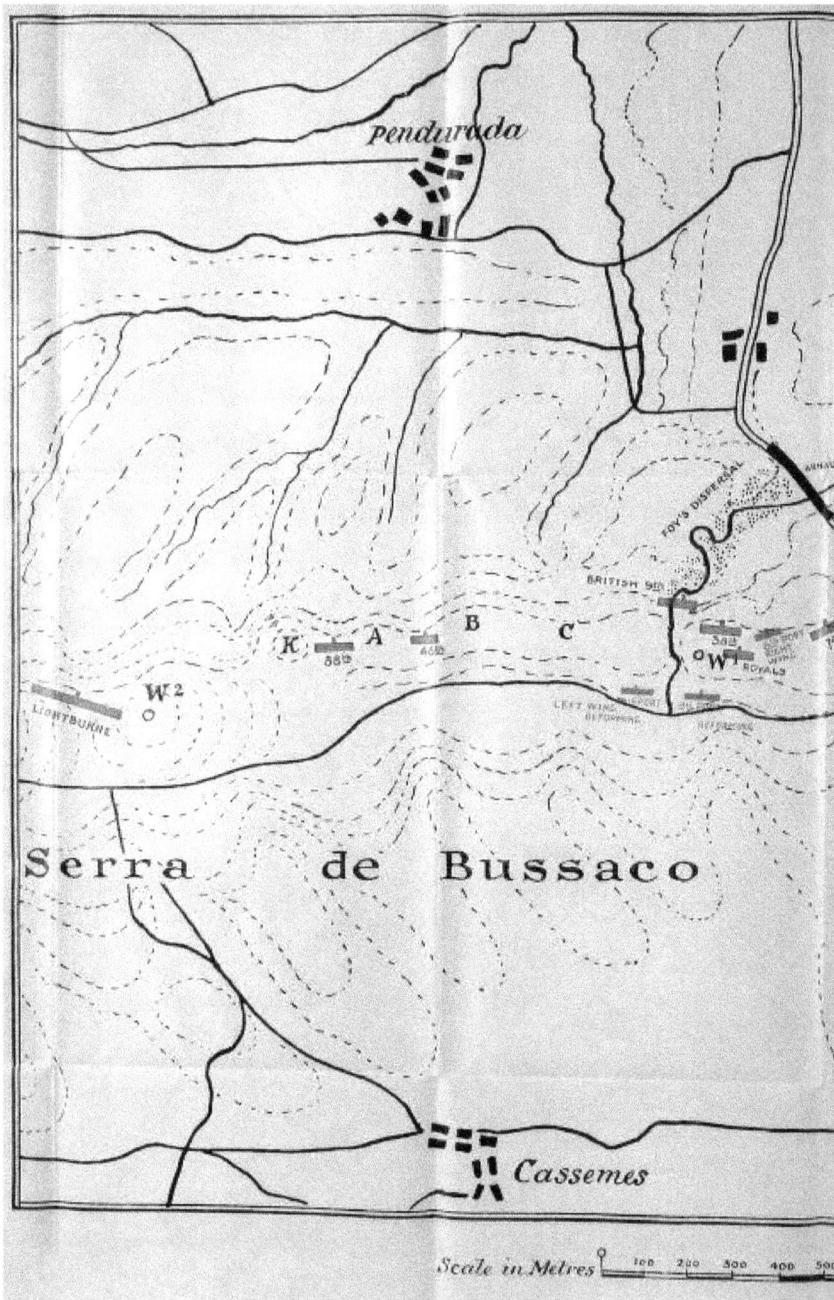

pendurada

FOY'S DISPERSAL

ARNAU

BRITISH 9TH

K A B C 582 W ROYALS
588 488 LEFT WING BEFORMING REFORMING

LIGHTBURNE W²

Serra de Bussaco

Cassemes

Scale in Metres 100 200 300 400 500

BATTLE OF BUSSACO
Sep. 27th 1810.

Foy's attack 3rd & last phase.
One Battalion beats seven.

S.Antonio
de Cantaro

BRITISH
PORTUGUESE
FRENCH

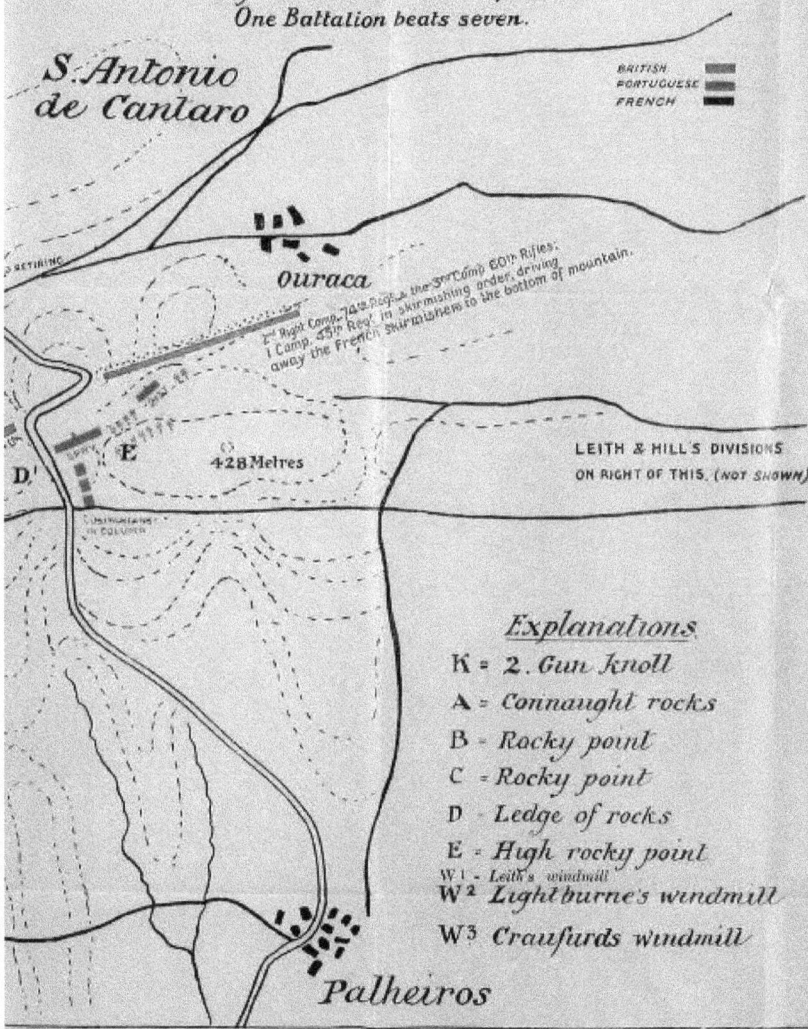

RETIRING

Ouraca

2 Right Comp. 74th Regts the 3rd Comp 60th Rifles.
I Camp. 45th Regt. in skirmishing order, driving
away the French Skirmishers to the bottom of mountain.

428 Metres

LEITH & HILL'S DIVISIONS
ON RIGHT OF THIS. (NOT SHOWN)

D'

E

HIGHLANDERS
IN COLUMN

Explanations

K = 2. Gun knoll
A = Connaught rocks
B = Rocky point
C = Rocky point
D = Ledge of rocks
E = High rocky point
W1 = Leith's windmill
W2 = Lightburne's windmill
W3 = Craufurds windmill

Palheiros

SWAN SONNENSCHEIN & CO LTD LONDON

1000   1500 METRES

pendurada

K   A   B   C

FOY

W1

8TH PORT. LT. INFANTRY

68TH WALLACE

LIGHTBURNE   W2

BARNES' BRIGADE

S e r r a   de   B u s s a c o

Cassemes

Scale in Metres   100   200   300   400   500

BATTLE OF BUSSACO

Sep. 27th 1810.

Foy's attack; 1st phase

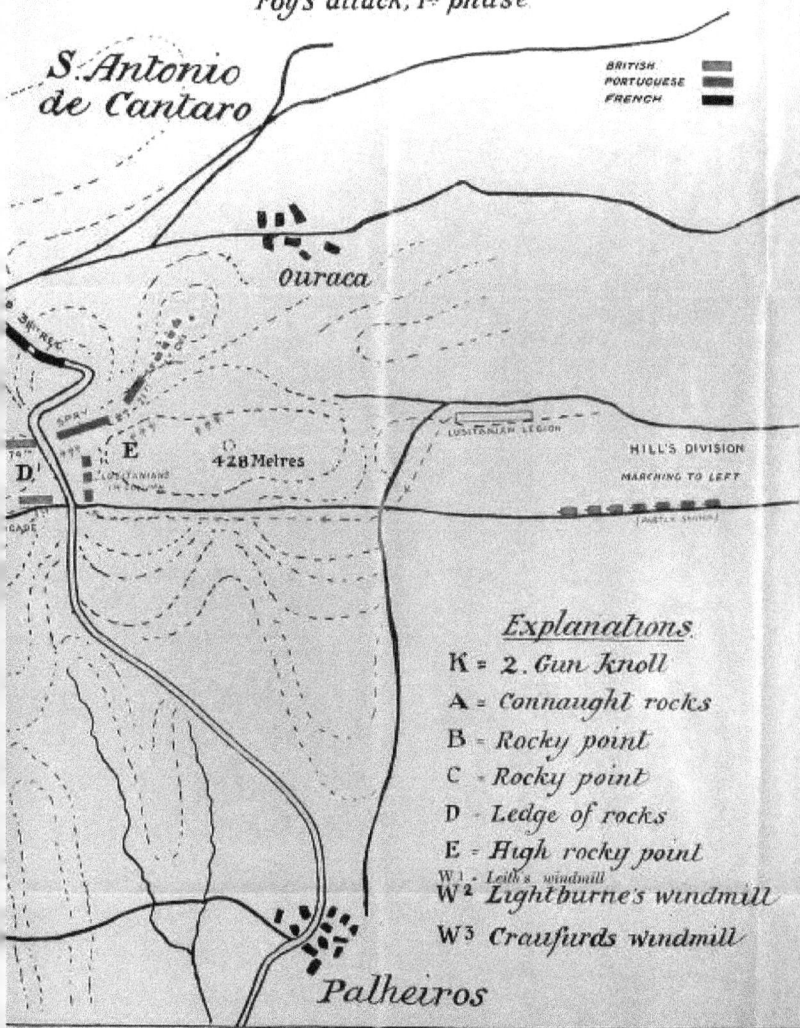

S. Antonio
de Cantaro

BRITISH
PORTUGUESE
FRENCH

Ouraca

LUSITANIAN LEGION

SPRY

E   428 Metres

HILL'S DIVISION

MARCHING TO LEFT

D'

LUSITANIANS

(PARTLY SEEN)

BRIGADE

Explanations.

K = 2 Gun knoll

A = Connaught rocks

B = Rocky point

C = Rocky point

D = Ledge of rocks

E = High rocky point

W 1 = Leith's windmill

W 2 Lightburne's windmill

W 3 Craufurds windmill

Palheiros

SWAN SONNENSCHEIN & CO. L.TD LONDON

1000   1500 METRES

pendurada

FOY

FRENCH RETREAT

FRENCH RETREAT
IN CONFUSION

PEPELE'S ADVANCE

GRAINDORGE

SARRUT

B

K

°A

C

LEFT WING 1887

SUPPORT
LEFT WING

MEADE 45TH

3 Guns 88TH

°W1

LIGHTBURNE

W2
°

Serra de Bussaco

Cassemes

Scale in Metres   100   200   300   400   5

BATTLE OF BUSSACO
Sep. 27th 1810.

Merle's attack on Picton (2nd phase,) and attack of 31st Leger on Pass Road (2nd phase)

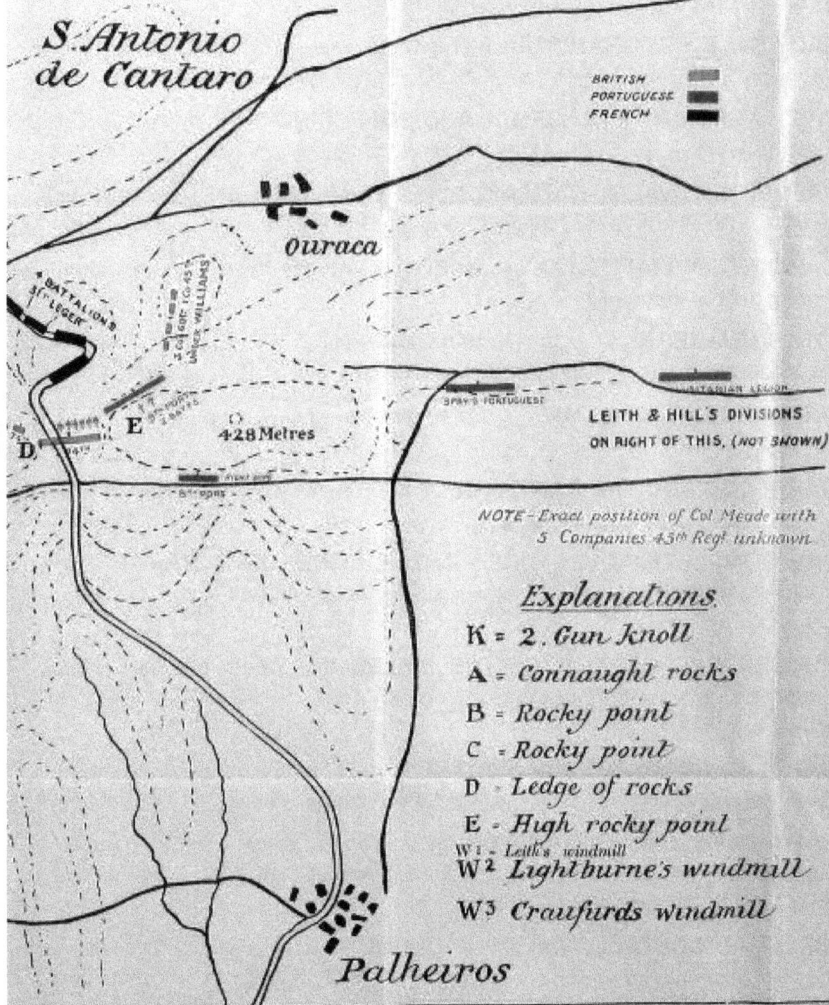

S. Antonio de Cantaro

BRITISH
PORTUGUESE
FRENCH

Ouraca

BATTALION 31st LEGER

2 COMPt TO 45th UNDER WILLIAMS

SPRY'S PORTUGUESE

LUSITANIAN LEGION

E

428 Metres

D

LEITH & HILL'S DIVISIONS
ON RIGHT OF THIS, (*NOT SHOWN*)

NOTE – Exact position of Col. Meade with 5 Companies 45th Regt. unknown.

Explanations.

K = 2. Gun knoll
A = Connaught rocks
B = Rocky point
C = Rocky point
D = Ledge of rocks
E = High rocky point
W1 = Leith's windmill
W2 Lightburne's windmill
W3 Craufurds windmill

Palheiros

SWAN SONNENSCHEIN & CO. LTD LONDON

1000   1500 METRES

LEONAUR

ALSO FROM LEONAUR

AVAILABLE IN SOFTCOVER OR HARDCOVER WITH DUST JACKET

THE FALL OF THE MOGHUL EMPIRE OF HINDUSTAN *by H. G. Keene*—By the beginning of the nineteenth century, as British and Indian armies under Lake and Wellesley dominated the scene, a little over half a century of conflict brought the Moghul Empire to its knees.

LADY SALE'S AFGHANISTAN *by Florentia Sale*—An Indomitable Victorian Lady's Account of the Retreat from Kabul During the First Afghan War.

THE CAMPAIGN OF MAGENTA AND SOLFERINO 1859 *by Harold Carmichael Wylly*—The Decisive Conflict for the Unification of Italy.

FRENCH'S CAVALRY CAMPAIGN *by J. G. Maydon*—A Special Correspondent's View of British Army Mounted Troops During the Boer War.

CAVALRY AT WATERLOO *by Sir Evelyn Wood*—British Mounted Troops During the Campaign of 1815.

THE SUBALTERN *by George Robert Gleig*—The Experiences of an Officer of the 85th Light Infantry During the Peninsular War.

NAPOLEON AT BAY, 1814 *by F. Loraine Petre*—The Campaigns to the Fall of the First Empire.

NAPOLEON AND THE CAMPAIGN OF 1806 *by Colonel Vachée*—The Napoleonic Method of Organisation and Command to the Battles of Jena & Auerstädt.

THE COMPLETE ADVENTURES IN THE CONNAUGHT RANGERS *by William Grattan*—The 88th Regiment during the Napoleonic Wars by a Serving Officer.

BUGLER AND OFFICER OF THE RIFLES *by William Green & Harry Smith*—With the 95th (Rifles) during the Peninsular & Waterloo Campaigns of the Napoleonic Wars.

NAPOLEONIC WAR STORIES *by Sir Arthur Quiller-Couch*—Tales of soldiers, spies, battles & sieges from the Peninsular & Waterloo campaigns.

CAPTAIN OF THE 95TH (RIFLES) *by Jonathan Leach*—An officer of Wellington's sharpshooters during the Peninsular, South of France and Waterloo campaigns of the Napoleonic wars.

RIFLEMAN COSTELLO *by Edward Costello*—The adventures of a soldier of the 95th (Rifles) in the Peninsular & Waterloo Campaigns of the Napoleonic wars.

www.ingramcontent.com/pod-product-compliance
Lightning Source LLC
Chambersburg PA
CBHW032041080426
42733CB00006B/157